# In the Dough

## Quick and easy recipes for your bread machine

### Beverlee & John Dwan

The J. B. Dough Company

# Acknowledgements

Graphic Design: Sassafras Studio
Contributing Writers: Kiki Walton, Patti Emmerson
Cover Photo: Palami Schroder Studio

## Special Thanks To

**Dolores Dwan**
for continual encouragement,
support and love.

## Family

**John, Brian, John III and Jenny**
and of course, Missy,
for working days and nights
and their love of bread
**Al & Terri Newman**
great friends to break bread with
**Dave and Pam Davis**
who got us started in all this
**Jack and Elsa Finwall**
family support and the name
**"In The Dough"**
**Bill, Jane and Frank Deaton**
for testing, tasting and proofing
**Favorite Recipes® Press**
**Bill Branch**
for starting this project
**Mary Cummings**
who kept this project alive with her wit, patience,
great ideas and much encouragement


Published by: The J. B. Dough Company
Copyright© The J. B. Dough Company
P.O. Box 557
St. Joseph, Michigan 49085-0557
(616) 983-1025
Library of Congress Number: 93-74985
ISBN: 0-87197-396-0
Edited and Manufactured in the United States of America by:
Favorite Recipes® Press
P.O. Box 305142
Nashville, Tennessee 37230
1-800-358-0560
First Printing: 1994  10,000 copies

# D e d i c a t i o n

This book is dedicated to the memory of my mom
**Betty Finwall**
who gave me my love of baking bread.
If only you were here to add your lovely Irish ways to it.
What fun we would have had baking
and researching this together.
Your memory will always be in my heart.

THESE THINGS I warmly wish for you—
   Someone to love,
   Some work to do,
A bit o'sun
A bit o' cheer
And a guardian angel
Always near.

*An Old Irish Greeting*

# Blending Traditions

As the ingredients of a good recipe join to create a wonderful bread, so did John and I combine our families' traditions and talents with our marriage. His family, the Dwans, left Ireland and settled in the Heartland. They chose a corner of Michigan where conditions are ideal for almost every type of fruit.

From this bounty, John's family originated award-winning sauces, preserves, jams, and jellies that friends and travelers alike collected from the roadside stand. Demand for the sweet bread toppings encouraged the Dwans to build a cannery that eventually spread their products all across the nation.

While John's family was busy making jams and jellies, my mother made five loaves of home-baked bread twice a week. For a delicious moment, the city of Chicago vanished as the smells and steam rising from the piping hot slices smothered in sweet creamery butter flooded our taste buds and disappeared into our mouths.

With my love for fresh bread and John's passion for fruit preserves, we have a marriage made in heaven. Like a great recipe though, we needed to have it kneaded a bit by a little Irish luck, Midwest opportunity, and answering the "knock at the door."

Four years ago, before bread making machines became the rage, an old friend of John's asked us why, with all the latest in Kitchen equipment, we didn't have a Bread Maker. We responded that I make my own Homemade Bread from my mother's recipe. He suggested with John's background we could come up with a recipe for a manufacturing company that wanted to include a bread mix with its bread making machines. Fifty-six combinations later, I finally was able to get my mother's classic white bread formula to perform to my satisfaction in that machine! When we succeeded, the manufacturer asked us to start shipping. In the midst of, and out of, all those flour sacks and yeast packets, The J. B. Dough Company was born.

Now, seventeen bread mixes later, and with more on the way, our small company continues to grow tremendously. Because I expect perfection of myself and because we named the company after our two sons, John III and Brian—my values run as deep as my Midwest roots— J. B. Dough breads are to look and taste absolutely delicious each and every time you bake a loaf. We use only the finest ingredients, allowing no shortcuts in quality, so that you can be assured of excellence in baking and mouthwatering performance in every slice.

The only time- or energy-saving cuts are made for you—all you have to do is add water to the perfectly prepared mix, bake and enjoy!

Some may say that a bread machine compromises the heritage of home-baked breads, but I see them as a blessing. For too long, children have grown up never knowing the excitement of baking bread, and adults have forgotten the fun and fragrance of a warm kitchen and the ambiance that is created as the bread bakes.

I do not believe that you should feel limited by a bread machine. It just does the hard, time-consuming job so that you can have the time to savor the shaping and baking process. This cookbook is filled with simple and easy ways that you, your bread machine, and our mixes can work together to give you greater freedom in baking creations without the pitfalls of failed experimentations and baking embarrassments. Using our mixes in your machine, you can produce beautiful breads each and every time.

**Dwan Canning Company fruit stand, circa 1940**

Jams, jellies, preserves and fruit were sold at the
roadside stand in St. Joseph, Michigan.

## Give thanks for bread . . .

Remember how much you loved to visit grandma's kitchen when all the family gathered together for a special occasion or holiday? The entire house was filled with the warm aroma of freshly baked bread. Nothing could compare to the happiness and tenderness found in that comfy kitchen immersed in the inviting smells and smiles that baking bread inspires.

How can we create that much-needed closeness in today's hectic world? J. B. Dough has the answers. Instead of all of the time it takes to knead and prepare the dough, use one of today's fantastic bread machines. What about all the wonderful recipes that grandma knew by heart? Use J. B. Dough's marvelous convenient mixes and this creative cookbook to transform your kitchen from a rushing, plastic, impersonal room, to an enticing, exciting fun-filled family world of real togetherness.

We would like to invite you to bake bread and bring love and laughter to you and yours.

# Contents

# Food Guide Pyramid

## A Guide To Daily Food Choices

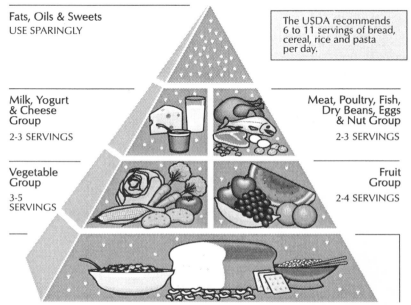

Fats, Oils & Sweets
USE SPARINGLY

The USDA recommends
6 to 11 servings of bread,
cereal, rice and pasta
per day.

Milk, Yogurt
& Cheese
Group

2-3 SERVINGS

Meat, Poultry, Fish,
Dry Beans, Eggs
& Nut Group

2-3 SERVINGS

Vegetable
Group

3-5
SERVINGS

Fruit
Group

2-4 SERVINGS

Source: U.S. Department of Agriculture/U.S. Department of
Health and Human Services

Bread, Cereal
Rice & Pasta Group

6-11 SERVINGS

Use the Food Guide Pyramid to help you eat better
every day . . . the Dietary Guidelines way. Start with
plenty of Breads, Cereals, Rice, and Pasta; Vegetables; and
Fruits. Add two to three servings from the Milk group and
two to three servings from the Meat group.

Each of these food groups provides some, but not all,
of the nutrients you need. No one food group is more
important than another—for good health you need them
all. Go easy on fats, oils and sweets, the foods in the small
tip of the Pyramid.

# All About Bread

## Not By Flour Alone

### *Salt and Sugar*

Salt gives flavor and inhibits the yeast from growing and adding too much gas. Sugar helps to feed the yeast.

### *Yeast*

Yeast is a leavening agent that is made up of thousands of tiny living plants. When given moisture, warmth and food, yeast will grow and release gas (carbon dioxide) which makes dough rise. To maximize yeast performance, careful measurement of other ingredients is required. Treat the yeast like a newborn baby. If the temperature is too high, it will kill the yeast. If it's too low, it will not activate the yeast.

### *Gluten*

The higher the gluten in bread the higher the bread will rise. Gluten is not needed as much in lighter breads. Add some to denser breads such as pumpernickel, rye and whole wheat. This is done for you in our J. B. Dough mixes.

### *Eggs*

When adding eggs to a recipe be sure they are at room temperature. You may eliminate the yolk if you're watching your cholesterol. Medium-sized eggs work well in bread recipes. Never use eggs in recipes that require non-refrigeration for long periods of time.

### *Fruits*

When adding fresh fruit or vegetables be sure to reduce your liquid amount. Apples and zucchini, for example, add a lot of moisture.

### *Rye*

Bread made from rye flour has a good flavor and will remain fresh longer than ordinary bread.

### *Herbs*

When adding herbs, substitute 1 teaspoon dry for 1 tablespoon fresh.

# Getting in Shape

### Kneading

Sometimes the plastic kneading paddles are difficult to remove from the pan when the dough sticks to them. Spray the paddle and hole with a vegetable spray. Never spray the pan. It will cause the dough to slip around too much and when baked will build up on the pan and become sticky. Be careful to spray just the paddle.

### Create a Design

Create old standards or original designs on loaves. Slash bread 3 times on a diagonal design or tree 1 long slash down the middle and then 2 slashes on an angle on each side. Or create any design and then brush with egg wash and sprinkle with oats, herbs or seeds. Or make a cut-out stencil using index stock. Use three leaves, or letters or use your own imagination. Sprinkle with flour and bake as directed.

### Braiding

To braid, divide bread into thirds. Roll each piece 12 inches long. Press ends together and then braid it. Leave it long, or roll into a circle and let rise in prepared pan for 1 hour and bake as directed.

### Round Loaves

Shape dough into a round loaf and place onto a prepared cookie sheet or 10-inch round cake pan. Brush top with water and sprinkle with flour. Using a sharp knife, mark top with a crisscross pattern. Let rise 1 hour and bake at 350 degrees for 25 to 30 minutes.

# The Bread Box

### After It's Baked

Keep bread fresh. Bread should sit out to be admired. Place it in a basket as a centerpiece or on a kitchen counter after it is cut or at the end of the day; then store in plastic. I give bread away in a basket and place the plastic bag underneath to be used to store the bread later. The Europeans do not put fresh bread in a plastic bag. It makes it soft.

### Storing Bread

Always cool bread completely. Store in a plastic bag. Store in a cool dry place for 2 or 3 days. Do not refrigerate baked yeast bread, because the bread will dry out and become stale. To freeze, place completely cooled bread in a plastic bag. Label and date. Store in the freezer for up to 3 months. It takes about 1 hour to defrost a whole loaf or a few minutes for a slice.

# Just Loaves

# L o a v e s

## Apple-Raisin-Honey Loaf

Prepare bread mix following J. B. Dough package instructions. Add honey with liquid ingredients. Wait for the beep. Add apple and raisins. Bake at normal or light mode. Makes 1 loaf.

1 package
  J. B. Dough
  Whole Wheat
  Bread mix

1 tablespoon honey

1 apple, finely chopped

1/4 cup raisins

1 package
 J. B. Dough
 Whole Earth
 Bread mix

1 teaspoon honey

1/3 cup mashed banana

1/8 teaspoon cinnamon

1/4 cup chopped
 walnuts

## Banana-Walnut Bread

Prepare bread mix following J. B. Dough package instructions, adding honey to warm water. Set your machine on light bake. Add mashed banana, cinnamon and walnuts at the first beep. Bake at normal or light mode. Makes 1 loaf.

*Add all ingredients at the beginning if using hand method.*

*Use light setting on your machine when using a recipe with high content of sugar.*

*Makes a great gift when made into two miniature loaves baked in conventional oven.*

# L o a v e s

## Three-Cheese Bread

Prepare bread mix following J. B. Dough package instructions. At the first beep, add Cheddar and Swiss cheese. Bake on normal mode. Brush with mixture of egg and water and sprinkle with Parmesan cheese and parsley 5 minutes before cycle ends. Makes 1 loaf.

1 package
  J. B. Dough
  French Bread mix

1/2 cup shredded
  Cheddar cheese

1/2 cup shredded Swiss
  cheese

1 egg, beaten

1 tablespoon water

Grated Parmesan
  cheese to taste

Chopped parsley

## Three-Cheese Rolls

Set your machine on the dough mode or on the manual setting. Remove dough from machine. Divide into 16 portions; place in greased pie plate. May layer the 16 portions in a double layer in loaf pan to make cheese bubble loaf. Let rise in warm place for 1 hour; brush with mixture of egg and water. Sprinkle with Parmesan cheese and parsley. Bake at 350 degrees for 25 to 30 minutes or until brown. Serve warm.

1 package
 J. B. Dough
 Classic White
 Bread mix

3 tablespoons sugar

2 tablespoons baking
 cocoa

1/4 cup dried cherries

1/2 cup slivered
 almonds

Confectioners' sugar

*May also use dough
mode. Form into
your favorite shape
or place in your
favorite bread pan.*

# Chocolate-Cherry-Nut Loaf

Prepare bread mix following
J. B. Dough package instructions.
Add sugar and baking cocoa with dry
ingredients. Set your machine for
light mode. Wait for the beep to add
cherries and almonds. Bake at normal
or light mode. Remove loaf to wire
rack to cool. Slice. Cut each slice into
4 wedges; sprinkle with confectioners'
sugar. Serve with cherry preserves.
Makes 1 loaf.

# L o a v e s

## Cinnamon-Raisin-Nut Bread

Prepare bread mix following J. B. Dough package instructions. Add sugar and cinnamon with dry ingredients. Add honey with liquid ingredients. Wait for the beep. Add raisins and walnuts or pecans. Bake at normal or light mode. Makes 1 loaf.

1 package
J. B. Dough Classic White Bread mix

1 teaspoon sugar

1/4 teaspoon cinnamon

2 teaspoons honey

1/4 cup raisins

2 to 4 tablespoons chopped walnuts or pecans

*Add raisins and nuts last if following the conventional method.*

*May use J. B. Dough Classic White, Six Grain, Whole Earth or Wheat and Honey mix with this recipe.*

1 package
   J. B. Dough
   Classic White
   Bread mix

2 tablespoons brown
   sugar

1/4 cup chopped sugar-
   coated dates

1/4 cup chopped
   walnuts

*Also works great on
dough mode. Form into
your favorite shape or
place in your favorite
bread pan. Brush with
egg wash; sprinkle with
vanilla sugar. Let rise
in warm place for
1 hour. Bake at 350
degrees for 25 to 30
minutes or until brown.*

## Date-Nut Loaf

Prepare bread mix following
J. B. Dough package instructions.
Add brown sugar with dry ingredients.
Wait for the first beep. Add dates and
walnuts. Bake at normal or light
mode. Serve with Honey Butter.
Makes 1 loaf.

1/2 cup butter, softened

2 tablespoons honey

## Honey Butter

Beat butter and honey in mixing bowl
until smooth.

# L o a v e s

## Irish Brown Bread

Prepare bread mix following J. B. Dough package instructions using 100 cc water. Add buttermilk and honey with liquid ingredients. Wait for the beep. Add 1/3 cup caraway seeds and raisins. Bake at normal mode. Brush with mixture of egg and water and sprinkle with caraway seeds 5 minutes before cycle ends. May use dough mode and shape into round loaf using greased 10-inch round baking pan or place on baking sheet. Crisscross bread with sharp knife into desired pattern. Brush with mixture of egg and water; sprinkle with caraway seeds. Let rise in warm place for 1 hour. Bake at 350 degrees for 25 to 30 minutes or until brown. Makes 1 loaf.

1 package
   J. B. Dough Whole
   Wheat Bread mix

100 cc water

100 cc buttermilk, at
   room temperature

1 tablespoon honey

1/3 cup caraway seeds

1/2 cup golden raisins

1 egg, beaten

1 tablespoon water

May your blessings outnumber
   The shamrocks that grow
   And may trouble avoid you
Wherever you go.

*An Old Irish Greeting*

1 package
  J. B. Dough
  Sweet Bread mix

1 tablespoon lemon
  juice

1 teaspoon chopped
  dried lemon rind

1/2 cup confectioners'
  sugar

2 teaspoons water

1 teaspoon lemon juice

# Lemon Bread

Prepare bread mix following
J. B. Dough package instructions.
Add 1 tablespoon lemon juice with
liquid ingredients. Wait for the beep.
Add lemon rind. Bake at normal
mode. Remove loaf to wire rack to
cool. Drizzle with mixture of
confectioners' sugar, water and 1
teaspoon lemon juice; sprinkle with
fresh lemon zest. Serve with Lemon
Butter. Makes 1 loaf.

1/2 cup butter, softened

1 tablespoon lemon
  juice

1/2 teaspoon chopped
  lemon rind

2 tablespoons
  confectioners' sugar

# Lemon Butter

Beat butter, lemon juice, lemon
rind and confectioners' sugar in bowl,
mixing until creamy.

# L o a v e s

## Lemony Pistachio Bread

Prepare bread mix following J. B. Dough package instructions. Add lemon juice with liquid ingredients. Wait for the beep. Add pistachios and lemon zest. Bake at normal mode. Remove to wire rack to cool. Drizzle with Lemon Glaze. Serve with Lemon Butter (page 19) and tea. Makes 1 loaf.

1 package
   J. B. Dough
   French Bread mix

1/4 cup lemon juice

1/2 cup chopped
   pistachios

1 teaspoon lemon zest

Lemon Glaze

### Lemon Glaze

1/3 cup confectioners'
   sugar

2 tablespoons lemon
   juice

Combine confectioners' sugar and lemon juice in bowl; mix well.

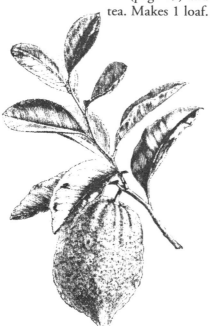

1 package
   J. B. Dough
   Whole Earth
   Bread mix

2 teaspoons parsley
   flakes

1/4 teaspoon onion
   powder

1 tablespoon molasses

1 tablespoon Cognac

1 tablespoon minced
   chives

1   2-ounce can
   chopped
   mushrooms, drained

1 egg, beaten

2 teaspoons water

Grated Parmesan
   cheese

Chopped parsley

# Mushroom Bread

Prepare bread mix following
J. B. Dough package instructions. Add
parsley flakes and onion powder with
dry ingredients. Add molasses and
Cognac with liquid ingredients.
Wait for beep.

Add chives and mushrooms. Bake
at normal mode. Brush with mixture of
egg and water and sprinkle with
Parmesan cheese and parsley 5 minutes
before cycle ends. Serve with
Mushroom Butter (page 118).
Makes 1 loaf.

# L o a v e s

## Calamata Olive Bread

Prepare bread mix following J. B. Dough package instructions. Add brown sugar and oregano with dry ingredients. Wait for the beep. Add olives and pine nuts. Bake at normal or light mode.

Brush with mixture of egg and water and sprinkle with Parmesan cheese and parsley 5 minutes before cycle ends. Makes 1 loaf.

1 package
  J. B. Dough
  Classic White
  Bread mix

1 teaspoon brown
  sugar

1/2 teaspoon oregano

1  8-ounce jar
  calamata olives,
  pitted, cut into
  quarters

1/4 cup chopped pine
  nuts, toasted
  (optional)

1 egg, beaten

1 tablespoon water

Grated Parmesan
  cheese

Chopped parsley

*May also use dough mode and shape into round peasant-type loaf.*

*Makes a great hostess gift accompanied with a bottle of wine.*

1 clove of garlic,
   chopped

1/2 medium green
   onion, chopped

2 tablespoons roasted
   sweet red bell
   pepper, chopped

1 tablespoon olive oil

1 package
   J. B. Dough
   Vienna Bread mix

1 teaspoon sugar

Cayenne pepper to
   taste

1 egg

1 tablespoon water

2 roasted red bell
   pepper strips

Chopped parsley

## Sweet Red Pepper Bread

Sauté garlic, green onion and
2 tablespoons chopped red pepper
in olive oil in skillet until tender.
Prepare bread mix following
J. B. Dough package instructions
for mixing dough. Add sugar and
cayenne pepper with dry ingredients.
Wait for the beep.

Add sautéed mixture. Bake at normal
or light mode. Brush with mixture of
egg and water and top with red pepper
strips and parsley 5 minutes before
cycle ends. Makes 1 loaf.

*This dough may be
baked in round loaf
pan or 10-inch cake
pan sprayed with
nonstick cooking spray.
Crisscross with sharp
knife; top with red
pepper strips. Let rise in
warm place for 1 hour.
Bake at 350 degrees for
25 to 30 minutes or
until brown.*

## Roasted Red Peppers

You can buy roasted red bell peppers
in the grocery store or roast your
own. Cut peppers into halves; remove
seeds. Place on baking sheet. Bake at
425 degrees for 20 to 25 minutes or
until skin is dark and bubbly. Place
in sealed plastic bag. Cool. Remove
skin; slice or chop.

# Loaves

## Pepperoni Pizza Bread

Prepare bread mix following J. B. Dough package instructions. Add oregano, garlic and basil with dry ingredients. Add olive oil with liquid ingredients. Wait for the beep. Add green onions, pepperoni, Parmesan cheese and provolone cheese. Bake at normal or light mode. Serve with your favorite spaghetti sauce over hot cooked pasta and with a salad. Makes 1 loaf.

|  |
|---|
| 1 package J. B. Dough Vienna Bread mix |
| 1/4 teaspoon oregano |
| 1 clove of garlic, finely chopped |
| 1/4 teaspoon basil |
| 1 tablespoon olive oil |
| 3 green onions, finely chopped |
| 1 ounce pepperoni, chopped |
| 2 tablespoons grated Parmesan cheese |
| 1/4 cup chopped provolone cheese |

*Broil thin slices of pizza bread for 3 to 5 minutes or until light brown on both sides and serve as an appetizer. Serve with chunky-style tomato sauce topped with fresh chopped cilantro.*

*Pizza bread also makes great croutons.*

## Savory Bacon Rye Bread

1 package
J. B. Dough
Country Rye
Bread mix

4 slices crisp-fried
bacon, crumbled

1 teaspoon caraway
seeds

1/2 teaspoon coarse
sea salt

Salt Wash

Caraway seeds to taste

Prepare bread mix following
J. B. Dough package instructions.
Wait for the first beep. Add bacon,
1 teaspoon caraway seeds and sea salt.
Bake at normal or light mode.

Add Salt Wash 5 minutes before end
of cycle; sprinkle with caraway seeds.
Makes 1 loaf.

*For dough mode, shape
into a ball; crisscross
with sharp knife. Place
on lightly greased baking
sheet. Brush with Salt
Wash; sprinkle with
caraway seeds. Let rise
in warm place for
1 hour. Bake at 350
degrees for 25 minutes
or until brown.*

## Salt Wash

2 tablespoons water

1 teaspoon salt

Microwave water and salt for 45
seconds in glass bowl; mix well.

# L o a v e s

## Country Rye with Orange Anise

Prepare bread mix following J. B. Dough package instructions, using 100 cc warm water. Add buttermilk with liquid ingredients. Add brown sugar with dry ingredients. Set your machine on light mode. Wait for the beep.

Add anise seeds and orange rind. Bake at normal or light mode. Brush with mixture of egg and water 5 minutes before cycle ends. Makes 1 loaf.

1 package
  J. B. Dough
  Country Rye
  Bread mix

100 cc warm water

100 cc warm
  buttermilk

2 teaspoons brown
  sugar

2 teaspoons anise seeds

1 tablespoon grated
  orange rind

1 egg

1 tablespoon water

*May use dough mode and use standard bread pan or shape dough into any desired shape.*

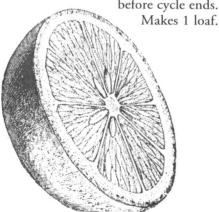

## Rosemary-Garlic Bread

1 package
  J. B. Dough
  Classic White
  Bread mix

1 tablespoon chopped
  fresh rosemary

2 cloves of garlic,
  finely chopped

1 tablespoon olive oil

1 egg, beaten

1 tablespoon water

Garlic salt to taste

Dried rosemary to taste

Prepare bread mix following
J. B. Dough package instructions. Add
1 tablespoon fresh rosemary with dry
ingredients. Add mixture of garlic
and olive oil with liquid ingredients.
Bake at normal or light mode. Brush
with mixture of egg and water and
sprinkle with garlic salt and dried
rosemary 5 minutes before cycle ends.
Makes 1 loaf.

*Use the dough mode
and shape the dough
into a round loaf.
Place in greased 10-
inch round bread pan.
Crisscross dough with
sharp knife; brush
with mixture of 1 egg
and 1 tablespoon water.
Sprinkle with garlic salt
and dried rosemary.
Let rise in warm place
for 1 hour. Bake at
350 degrees for 25 to
30 minutes.*

*Great for holiday giving.*

# L o a v e s

## Cinnamon Swirl Bread

Prepare bread mix following J. B. Dough package instructions. Set your machine on the dough mode or on the manual setting.

Remove dough from the bread machine. Roll into 8x12-inch rectangle on lightly floured surface. Drizzle with 3 tablespoons melted butter; sprinkle with mixture of sugar and cinnamon. Roll as for jelly roll, sealing ends.

Place seam side down in greased 5x9-inch loaf pan. Let rise in warm place for 1 hour. Bake at 350 degrees for 25 minutes. Let stand in pan for 10 minutes. Remove to wire rack; spread with 1 tablespoon butter. Makes 1 loaf.

---

1 package
    J. B. Dough
    Classic White
    Bread mix

3 tablespoons melted
    butter

3 tablespoons sugar

1/2 to 1 teaspoon
    cinnamon

1 tablespoon butter,
    softened

## Fanned Coconut-Orange-Lemon Loaf

1 package
  J. B. Dough
  Sweet Bread mix

2 tablespoons melted
  butter

1/4 cup sugar

1/4 cup flaked coconut

2 teaspoons grated
  lemon rind

2 teaspoons grated
  orange rind

1 egg, beaten

1 tablespoon water

Sugar to taste

Prepare bread mix following
J. B. Dough package instructions. Set
your machine on the dough mode or
on the manual setting.

Remove dough from bread machine.
Roll dough into 12x18-inch rectangle
on lightly floured surface. Drizzle with
melted butter. Sprinkle with mixture of
1/4 cup sugar, coconut, lemon rind and
orange rind.

Fold into 9x12-inch rectangle; cut
lengthwise into two 6x9-inch strips.
Stack; cut into 3x9-inch strips. Stack;
cut into six 1 1/2x3-inch strips.
Arrange in single layer side by side
filling side up in greased loaf pan.
Brush with mixture of egg and water;
sprinkle with sugar.

Let rise in warm place for 1 hour. Bake
at 350 degrees for 25 to 30 minutes or
until brown. Makes 1 loaf.

# L o a v e s

## Garlic Monkey Bread

Prepare bread mix following J. B. Dough package instructions. Set your machine on the dough mode or on the manual setting. Remove dough from bread machine. Divide dough into 16 portions. Roll each portion in mixture of melted butter, parsley, chives, onion powder, garlic powder and seasoned salt.

Layer in greased bundt pan; drizzle with remaining butter mixture. Let rise in warm place for 1 hour. Bake at 350 degrees for 25 minutes. Cool in pan for 10 minutes. Invert onto serving platter. Makes 1 loaf.

1 package
    J. B. Dough
    Classic White
    Bread mix

1/2 cup melted butter

2 teaspoons parsley
    flakes

1 tablespoon chopped
    fresh chives

3/4 teaspoon onion
    powder

3/4 teaspoon garlic
    powder

1/2 teaspoon seasoned
    salt

*Serve with homemade soup and a salad for a great fall dinner.*

1 package
   J. B. Dough
   Vienna Bread mix

1/4 cup melted butter

1 teaspoon parsley
   flakes

1 teaspoon onion
   powder

1/4 teaspoon garlic
   powder

1/2 teaspoon basil

1/4 teaspoon Italian
   seasoning

# Italian Herb Pull-Apart Bread

Prepare bread mix following
J. B. Dough package instructions. Set
your machine on the dough mode or
on the manual setting.

Remove dough from bread machine.
Divide dough into 12 to 16 portions.
Layer in greased bundt pan. Drizzle
with melted butter; sprinkle with
mixture of parsley, onion powder,
garlic powder, basil and Italian
seasoning.

Let rise in warm place for 1 hour.
Bake at 350 degrees for 25 to 30
minutes or until brown. Cool in pan
for 10 minutes. Invert onto serving
platter. Serve immediately.
Makes 1 loaf.

# L o a v e s

## Onion and Caraway Country Rye Bread

Prepare bread mix following J. B. Dough package instructions. Add brown sugar, onion flakes and 1 teaspoon caraway seeds with dry ingredients. Set your machine on the dough mode or on the manual setting.

Remove dough from bread machine. Shape into round loaf. Place in greased 10-inch round bread pan. Crisscross dough with sharp knife.

Microwave butter in microwave-safe dish until melted. Add onions; mix well. Microwave for 1 minute or until onions are tender; drain. Spoon onions over dough; sprinkle with caraway seeds. Let rise in warm place for 1 hour. Bake at 350 degrees for 25 to 30 minutes or until brown. Makes 1 loaf.

1 package
   J. B. Dough
   Country Rye
   Bread mix

1 tablespoon brown
   sugar

1 teaspoon onion flakes

1 teaspoon caraway
   seeds

2 tablespoons butter

1 small onion, finely
   chopped

2 green onions, finely
   chopped

Caraway seeds to taste

*Serve with ham and corn pudding.*

1 package
  J. B. Dough
  Vienna Bread mix

Sesame seeds to taste

## Italian Sesame Twist

Prepare bread mix following
J. B. Dough package instructions. Set
your machine on the dough mode or
on the manual setting.

Remove dough from bread machine.
Divide dough into 3 portions. Shape
into three 12-inch ropes. Braid the
ropes; seal the ends. Shape into
wreath on greased baking sheet, sealing
ends. Brush with water; sprinkle with
sesame seeds.

Let rise in warm place for 1 hour. Bake
at 350 degrees for 25 to 30 minutes or
until brown. Makes 1 loaf, as shown
on cover.

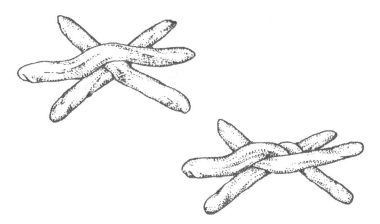

# Loaves

## Spinach-Cheese Bread

Prepare bread mix following J. B. Dough package instructions. Set your machine on the dough mode or on the manual setting.

Remove dough from bread machine. Roll into rectangle on lightly floured surface.

Microwave butter and garlic in microwave-safe dish for 30 seconds or until butter melts. Drizzle butter mixture over dough. Spread with mixture of spinach and Parmesan cheese; sprinkle with onion powder and basil. Roll as for jelly roll, sealing edge. Cut roll lengthwise with sharp knife or scissors forming 2 strips; turn filling side up. Twist strips together loosely.

Coil strip into circle, turning end under. Transfer with spatula to greased springform pan; dough does not touch edge of pan. Brush with mixture of egg and water; sprinkle with Parmesan cheese. Let rise in warm place for 1 hour. Bake at 350 degrees for 30 minutes or until brown. Makes 1 loaf, as shown on cover.

1 package
  J. B. Dough
  Classic White
  Bread mix

2 tablespoons butter

1 clove of garlic, finely chopped

1   10-ounce package frozen spinach, cooked, drained

1/3 cup grated Parmesan cheese

1/2 teaspoon onion powder

1/4 teaspoon basil

1 egg, beaten

1 tablespoon water

Grated Parmesan cheese to taste

# Brunch

# Brunch

## French Beignets

| | 1 package<br>J. B. Dough<br>Sweet Bread mix |
| | Peanut oil for deep frying |
| | Confectioners' sugar |

Prepare bread mix following J. B. Dough package instructions. Set your machine on the dough mode or on the manual setting.

Remove dough from machine. Roll dough to 1/2-inch thickness on floured surface. Cut into square pieces. Deep-fry several at a time in 5 inches 350-degree hot oil until brown on both sides. Drain on paper towels; dust with confectioners' sugar. Makes 12 beignets.

*Do not allow the dough to rise before deep frying. Rising will occur as beignets cook.*

1 package
 J. B. Dough Whole
 Earth Bread mix

2 teaspoons sugar

1 teaspoon cinnamon

2 tablespoons sugar

Confectioners' Sugar
 Glaze

## Confectioners' Sugar Glaze

1/2 cup confectioners'
 sugar

1 tablespoon water

Combine confectioners' sugar and water in small bowl; mix well.

# Brian's Cinnamon Bubble Loaf

Prepare bread mix following J. B. Dough package instructions. Add 2 teaspoons sugar with dry ingredients. Set your machine on the dough mode or on the manual setting.

Remove dough from bread machine. Divide dough into 16 to 20 portions. Roll each in mixture of cinnamon and remaining 2 tablespoons sugar. Place in well-greased 5x9-inch loaf pan. Let rise for 1 hour.

Bake at 350 degrees for 25 to 30 minutes or until loaf tests done. Let cool in pan for 10 minutes. Remove to wire rack to cool completely. Drizzle with Confectioners' Sugar Glaze. If you can't wait for the loaf to cool, sprinkle with confectioners' sugar instead. Makes 1 loaf.

# B r u n c h

## Blintzes

Trim crust from bread. Cut loaf into slices. Roll each slice with rolling pin to flatten. Cream sugar, cream cheese and egg yolk in bowl. Spread each bread slice with cream cheese mixture. Roll as for jelly roll.

Cut each roll into halves. Roll in mixture of melted butter, 1 tablespoon sugar and cinnamon. Arrange on baking sheet. Bake at 350 degrees for 4 to 5 minutes or until crisp and golden brown. Makes 24 servings.

1 loaf
   J. B. Dough
   Classic White Bread

$1/2$ cup sugar

8 ounces cream cheese, softened

1 egg yolk

1 cup melted butter

1 tablespoon sugar

$1/4$ teaspoon cinnamon

Dash of almond extract

# Nutty Sticky Buns

1 package
J. B. Dough
Whole Earth
Bread mix

2 teaspoons brown
sugar

1/2 cup melted butter
or margarine

1 1/2 cups packed
brown sugar

1/2 cup chopped pecans

*This recipe works well for Saturday mornings. Prepare everything on Friday night. Do not let rise. Chill, loosely covered, overnight. Remove cover in morning; place in cold oven. Bake at 350 degrees for 25 to 30 minutes or until brown. Really smells great on those cold midwestern fall mornings and gets everyone out of bed with no problem, especially growing teenaged boys.*

Prepare bread mix following J. B. Dough package instructions. Add 2 teaspoons brown sugar with dry ingredients. Set your machine on the dough mode or on the manual setting.

Remove dough from bread machine. Roll dough into 15x20-inch rectangle on floured surface.

Combine butter and remaining 1 1/2 cups brown sugar in small bowl; mix well. Spread evenly over dough to within 1 inch of edge. Roll tightly as for jelly roll from long end; seal edge and ends. Cut into 1-inch slices.

Sprinkle pecans over bottom of generously greased 9x13-inch baking pan. Arrange rolls cut side down in prepared pan. Let rise for 1 hour. Bake at 350 degrees for 25 minutes. Cool in pan for 2 minutes. Invert onto serving platter. Makes 8 servings.

# B r u n c h

## Banana-Walnut French Toast

Cut loaf into 8 thick slices. Then cut each slice in half on an angle. Place slices in shallow dish. Beat eggs with milk and vanilla in bowl. Pour egg mixture over slices. Let stand until egg mixture is absorbed by bread slices.

Preheat griddle or large skillet. Fry bread slices in butter for 2 to 3 minutes on each side or until golden brown, turning once. Place on serving platter. Repeat with remaining slices. Sprinkle with confectioners' sugar. Makes 8 servings.

1 loaf Banana-Walnut Bread (page 13)

3 eggs

1/2 cup milk

1 teaspoon vanilla extract

Butter or margarine

Confectioners' sugar

*May substitute 3 egg whites and 1 egg yolk for 3 whole eggs.*

8 slices of your
favorite bread

4 eggs

1¹/₂ cups milk

¹/₄ cup maple syrup

1 tablespoon canola oil

1 tablespoon butter

Confectioners' sugar

*"Bread is the one food
one can eat thrice daily
and not tire of."*

## Favorite French Toast

Cut bread slices into triangles. Arrange in medium rectangular baking dish. Beat eggs with milk and maple syrup in bowl. Pour over bread. Let stand for 10 to 15 minutes.

Heat canola oil and butter in large skillet until bubbly. Add bread triangles. Fry until golden brown on both sides, turning once. Remove to serving platter. Repeat with remaining triangles. Sprinkle with confectioners' sugar. Serve with warm maple syrup and Honey Butter (page 17). Makes 8 servings.

# B r u n c h

## Freezer Orange French Toast

Slice loaf as desired. Reserve end slices to make crumbs and set aside for another purpose. Beat eggs with milk, orange juice, sugar, orange rind, cinnamon and salt in bowl. Dip bread slices into egg mixture; arrange on greased baking sheet, leaving space between slices. Drizzle remaining egg mixture slowly over slices.

Freeze, covered, until firm. Remove frozen slices from baking sheet. Stack frozen slices between waxed paper; place in plastic freezer bags. Store in freezer for up to 6 months.

Preheat oven to 425 degrees. Remove frozen slices from freezer. Brush one side with melted butter. Place butter side down on baking sheet sprayed with nonstick cooking spray. Bake for 10 to 15 minutes. Brush with melted butter. Bake for 5 minutes longer or until golden brown. Remove to serving plate. Sprinkle with confectioners' sugar. Garnish with fresh orange slices. Serve with maple syrup. Makes 10 servings.

1 loaf of your favorite J. B. Dough bread

3 eggs

1/2 cup milk

1/2 cup orange juice

2 tablespoons sugar

1 teaspoon grated orange rind

1/4 teaspoon cinnamon

Dash of salt

1/3 cup melted butter or margarine

*May substitute 3 egg whites and 1 egg yolk for 3 whole eggs.*

# Brunch

## Breakfast Sandwiches

1 package
   J. B. Dough English
   Muffin Bread mix

4 eggs

8 cooked breakfast
   sausage patties, well
   drained

1 cup shredded
   Cheddar cheese

*This is great when you have guests for breakfast. It is easy to do a lot all at once and keep warm. The bread can be made the day before.*

Prepare bread mix following J. B. Dough package instructions. Set your machine on the dough mode or on the manual setting.

Remove dough from bread machine. Divide into 2 portions on lightly floured surface. Shape each portion into 10 to 12-inch log. Place on greased baking sheet. Let rise for 1 hour. Bake at 350 degrees for 25 minutes. Let stand until cool. Cut into 16 slices.

Beat eggs in bowl. Pour into preheated skillet sprayed with nonstick cooking spray. Cook until soft scrambled. Place half the bread slices on baking sheet. Add sausage patties, eggs, cheese and remaining bread slices. Bake at 350 degrees for 4 to 5 minutes or until cheese is melted. Makes 8 sandwiches.

# B r u n c h

## Kolaches

Prepare bread mix following J. B. Dough package instructions. Set your machine on the dough mode or on the manual setting.

Remove dough from bread machine. Divide into 16 portions on lightly floured surface. Shape each into a ball. Arrange about 3 inches apart on greased baking sheet. Flatten each to 2¹/2-inch circle. Let rise, covered, for 45 minutes or until doubled in bulk. Make indentation in center of each with thumb. Fill each indentation with about 2 teaspoons desired preserves. Brush lightly with milk. Bake at 350 degrees for 10 to 12 minutes or until golden brown. Cool. Sprinkle with confectioners' sugar. Makes 16 kolaches.

1 package
  J. B. Dough
  Sweet Bread mix

**Fruit preserves**

**Milk**

**Confectioners' sugar**

*Kolaches are an eastern European favorite, traditionally shaped into circles. The circle is a symbol of good luck, prosperity and eternity.*

1 package
   J. B. Dough Classic
   White Bread mix

1/2 cup sugar

1 teaspoon cinnamon

Sugar

1 teaspoon cinnamon

1/2 cup melted butter
   or margarine

*After spooning melted butter over dough balls, you may place in refrigerator overnight and bake in the morning.*

# Easy Monkey Bread

Prepare bread mix following J. B. Dough package instructions. Set your machine on the dough mode or on the manual setting.

Remove dough from bread machine. Divide dough into 16 portions on lightly floured surface. Shape each into a ball. Roll in mixture of 1/2 cup sugar and 1 teaspoon cinnamon. Place in greased bundt pan.

Pour any remaining cinnamon-sugar mixture into 2-cup measure. Add enough additional sugar to bring mixture to 1-cup level. Stir in 1 teaspoon cinnamon and melted butter. Spoon over dough balls.

Let rise for 1 hour. Bake at 350 degrees for 30 minutes. Let stand for 10 minutes. Invert onto serving plate. Serve warm. Makes 16 servings.

# B r u n c h

## Quick Mini Breakfast Pizza

Slice loaf as desired. Arrange slices on ungreased baking sheet. Place under broiler for 1 to 2 minutes or until toasted. Turn slices over. Broil for 1 minute or until toasted.

Sprinkle with sausage, cheeses and green onions. Broil for 2 to 3 minutes or until cheeses melt. Makes 12 servings.

1 loaf
   J. B. Dough English
   Muffin Bread

1/2 cup cooked drained
   sausage

1/2 cup shredded
   mozzarella cheese

1/2 cup shredded
   Cheddar cheese

1/4 cup grated
   Parmesan cheese

1/4 cup finely chopped
   green onions

*This is great for when your kids have sleep-overs. They can even help to sprinkle on the toppings. I cook the sausage in the microwave and buy the cheese already shredded—the less work in the morning, the better. Serve with a pitcher of orange juice in the summer and hot chocolate in the winter.*

1 package
   J. B. Dough Classic
   White Bread mix

2 tablespoons melted
   butter

1/3 cup cherry preserves

3 tablespoons toasted
   sliced almonds

Vanilla Glaze

## Vanilla Glaze

1/2 cup confectioners'
   sugar

1 1/2 teaspoons butter,
   softened

1/4 teaspoon vanilla
   extract

1 to 2 teaspoons milk

Blend confectioners'
sugar, softened butter,
vanilla and enough
milk to make of
drizzling consistency in
small bowl.

# Cherry-Almond Coffee Cake

Prepare bread mix following
J. B. Dough package instructions. Set
your machine on the dough mode or
on the manual setting.

Remove dough from bread machine.
Roll into rectangle on lightly floured
surface. Brush with melted butter.
Spread with preserves. Sprinkle with
almonds. Roll as for jelly roll from
long edge. Seal edge. Cut into halves
lengthwise.

Coil loosely cut side up beginning in
center of well greased springform pan.
Let rise for 1 hour. Bake at 350
degrees for 25 to 30 minutes or
until golden brown. Remove to wire
rack to cool. Drizzle Vanilla Glaze
over cooled coffee cake. Sprinkle
with additional almonds.
Makes 1 coffee cake.

# Brunch

## Walnut Coffee Cake

Prepare bread mix following J. B. Dough package instructions. Set your machine on the dough mode or on the manual setting.

Remove dough from bread machine. Roll into 15x18-inch rectangle on lightly floured surface. Spread melted butter to within 1 inch of edges. Sprinkle with brown sugar, cinnamon and 2 tablespoons walnuts. Roll as for jelly roll from long edge. Seal edge and ends. Cut lengthwise into halves. Twist strips together with cut edges on top. Shape into circle. Place in greased springform pan. Brush with mixture of egg and water.

Let rise for 1 hour. Bake at 350 degrees for 25 to 30 minutes or until golden brown. Remove to wire rack to cool completely. Drizzle with mixture of confectioners' sugar and milk. Sprinkle with 1 tablespoon walnuts. Makes 1 coffee cake.

1 package
    J. B. Dough
    Sweet Bread mix

2 tablespoons melted
    butter or margarine

2 tablespoons brown
    sugar

1/2 teaspoon cinnamon

2 tablespoons chopped
    walnuts

1 egg, beaten

1 tablespoon water

1/2 cup confectioners'
    sugar

4 teaspoons milk

1 tablespoon walnuts

1 package
   J. B. Dough
   Sweet Bread mix

1 egg white

3/4 cup confectioners'
   sugar

1/2 cup almond paste

1 egg

1 tablespoon water

Sliced almonds

Vanilla Sugar

# Bear Claws

Prepare bread mix following
J. B. Dough package instructions. Set
your machine on the dough mode or
on the manual setting.

Remove dough from bread machine.
Divide into 2 portions on lightly
floured surface. Roll each into
12-inch square. Cut each square
into three 4-inch wide strips.

Beat egg white, confectioners' sugar
and almond paste in bowl until
well blended. Spread 2 tablespoons
almond filling down center of each
strip; fold over lengthwise to enclose
filling, sealing edge. Cut each strip into
three 4-inch pieces. Make 4 or
5 cuts from edge to but not through
fold. Arrange 1 1/2 inches apart on
ungreased baking sheets, curving
slightly to separate cuts.

Let rise in warm place for 1 hour or
until doubled in bulk. Brush lightly
with egg beaten with 1 tablespoon
water. Sprinkle with almonds and
Vanilla Sugar (page 89). Bake at 350
degrees for 15 minutes or until golden
brown. Remove to wire rack. Serve
warm. Makes 18 bear claws.

# B r u n c h

## Sweet Apricot Ring

Prepare bread mix following J. B. Dough package instructions. Add sugar and 2 teaspoons lemon rind. Set your machine on the dough mode or on the manual setting.

Remove dough from bread machine. Roll into rectangle on lightly floured surface. Spread melted butter to within 1 inch of edges.

Microwave apricot preserves in microwave-safe bowl on Medium for 1 minute or until melted. Spread over butter. Roll as for jelly roll from long edge. Place on greased baking sheet. Shape into ring; pinch ends together.

Cut 1/3 of the way through ring at 1 1/2-inch intervals. Turn each slice cut side up. Let rise for 1 hour. Bake at 350 degrees for 25 minutes or until golden brown. Cool on wire rack. Drizzle Sour Cream Glaze over coffee cake. Makes 1 coffee cake.

1 package
J. B. Dough Classic White Bread mix

1 tablespoon sugar

2 teaspoons grated lemon rind

2 tablespoons melted butter

3 tablespoons apricot preserves

Sour Cream Glaze

### Sour Cream Glaze

2 tablespoons butter

1/4 cup sugar

1/4 cup sour cream

1 teaspoon grated lemon rind

Microwave 2 tablespoons butter and 1/4 cup sugar in glass microwave-safe bowl for 1 minute. Blend in sour cream. Add 1 teaspoon lemon rind.

1 package
J. B. Dough Classic
White Bread mix

2 teaspoons brown
sugar

2 tablespoons melted
butter

1/2 cup packed brown
sugar

1/2 teaspoon cinnamon

1/2 teaspoon nutmeg

1 or 2 golden
Delicious apples,
peeled, thinly sliced

1/2 cup confectioners'
sugar

3 teaspoons water
or milk

# Cinnamon and Sugar Apple Ring

Prepare bread mix following
J. B. Dough package instructions.
Add 2 teaspoons brown sugar. Set
your machine on the dough mode or
on the manual setting.

Remove dough from bread machine.
Roll into rectangle on lightly floured
surface. Brush with butter to within
1 inch of edges. Sprinkle with
mixture of 1/2 cup brown sugar,
cinnamon and nutmeg. Roll as for
jelly roll. Seal edges and ends.

Shape into ring on greased baking
sheet; seal ends together. Make
1/2-inch deep cut every 1 1/2 inches
around ring using serrated knife.
Press 2 or 3 apple slices into each
cut. Let rise for 1 hour. Bake at 350
degrees for 25 to 30 minutes or until
golden brown. Cool on wire rack.
Drizzle with mixture of confectioners'
sugar and water. Makes 1 coffee cake.

# B r u n c h

## Country Apple Coffee Cake

Prepare bread mix following J. B. Dough package instructions. Add 2 teaspoons brown sugar. Set your machine on the dough mode or on the manual setting.

Remove dough from bread machine. Roll into rectangle on lightly floured surface. Brush with melted butter. Sprinkle 1/3 cup brown sugar and cinnamon to within 1 inch of edges. Add layers of chopped apple and pecans.

Roll as for jelly roll from long edge. Seal edge. Slash down length of roll exposing a portion of filling. Shape into circle with slash on top in greased springform pan. Let rise for 1 hour. Brush with mixture of egg and 1 teaspoon water. Let rise for 1 hour. Bake at 350 degrees for 30 minutes. Cool for 10 minutes.

Remove from pan to cool completely on wire rack. Drizzle with mixture of confectioners' sugar and 2 to 3 teaspoons water or sprinkle with confectioners' sugar. Makes 1 coffee cake.

---

1 package
   J. B. Dough Classic
   White Bread mix

2 teaspoons brown
   sugar

2 tablespoons melted
   butter

1/3 cup packed brown
   sugar

1/4 teaspoon cinnamon

11/2 cups finely
   chopped apple

1/2 cup pecans

1 egg, beaten

1 teaspoon water

1/2 cup confectioners'
   sugar

2 to 3 teaspoons water

1 package
  J. B. Dough Classic
  White Bread mix

3 tablespoons sugar

2 tablespoons baking
  cocoa

2 teaspoons cappucino
  dry instant coffee
  mix

1/2 cup slivered
  almonds

Confectioners' sugar

*This is great for after dinner or Sunday brunch when served with flavored coffees. My favorite is chocolate-raspberry.*

# Chocolate-Almond Cappucino Bread

Prepare bread mix following J. B. Dough package instructions for mixing dough. Add sugar, baking cocoa, instant coffee and almonds. Set your machine for light mode because of the high sugar content. Bake on normal or light mode. Let cool. Slice and sprinkle with confectioners' sugar.

Or, if you use the dough mode, remove dough from bread machine. Divide into 2 portions on lightly floured surface. Shape each into 12-inch rope. Twist ropes together loosely; pinch ends together.

Place on greased baking sheet. Let rise for 1 hour. Bake at 350 degrees for 25 to 30 minutes. Cool on wire rack. Sprinkle with confectioners' sugar. Makes 1 loaf.

# B r u n c h

## Sweet Sunday Bread

Prepare bread mix following J. B. Dough package instructions. Add lemon rind. Set your machine on the dough mode or on the manual setting.

Remove dough from bread machine. Roll into 3/4-inch thick rectangle on lightly floured surface. Brush with melted butter. Mix apple, almonds, raisins, honey and cinnamon in small bowl. Sprinkle over dough.

Roll as for jelly roll from long edge. Seal edge. Shape seam side down into ring on greased baking sheet. Cut from outer edge to but not through center at 1-inch intervals. Separate slices enough to twist slightly and lay cut side down overlapping slightly.

Let rise for 1 hour in warm oven. Turn on oven. Bake at 350 degrees for 25 minutes. May drizzle warm rolls with confectioners' sugar glaze. Makes 1 loaf.

| |
|---|
| 1 package J. B. Dough Sweet Bread mix |
| 1 teaspoon freshly grated lemon rind |
| 2 tablespoons melted butter |
| 1/2 cup chopped apple |
| 1/2 cup slivered almonds |
| 1/4 cup raisins |
| 2 tablespoons honey |
| 1 teaspoon cinnamon |

1/4 cup raisins

50 cc rum

1 package
   J. B. Dough Classic
   White Bread mix

150 cc warm water

1 teaspoon dried or
   fresh lemon zest

1 egg, beaten

1 teaspoon water

Confectioners' sugar

*Serve this loaf warm with your favorite breakfast omelet. It is great for after-church Sunday brunch and with very little effort.*

# Rum-Raisin Loaf

Soak raisins in a small amount of rum for several minutes. Drain, reserving rum. Prepare bread mix following J. B. Dough package instructions, using warm water and reserved rum. Add lemon zest. Set your machine on the dough mode or on the manual setting. Add raisins at the first beep.

Remove dough from bread machine. Place in lightly greased loaf pan. Slash dough 3 times. Brush with mixture of egg and water. Place in refrigerator overnight. Place in oven. Turn oven on to 350 degrees. Bake for 30 minutes. Remove loaf to wire rack. Dust with confectioners' sugar. Makes 1 loaf.

# Brunch

## Whole Earth Cinnamon Rolls

Prepare bread mix following J. B. Dough package instructions. Add 1 teaspoon brown sugar. Set your machine on the dough mode or on the manual setting.

Remove dough from bread machine. Roll into rectangle on lightly floured surface. Spread melted butter to within 1 inch of edges. Sprinkle with 1/4 cup brown sugar and cinnamon.

Roll as for jelly roll from long edge. Seal edge. Cut into 1-inch slices. Arrange cut side down on greased baking sheet. Let rise in warm place for 1 hour.

Bake at 350 degrees for 20 to 25 minutes or until golden brown. Let stand for 5 minutes. Remove from pan. Sprinkle with confectioners' sugar or drizzle with Confectioners' Sugar Glaze (page 37). Makes 12 servings.

1 package
J. B. Dough Whole Earth Bread mix

1 teaspoon brown sugar

3 tablespoons melted butter or margarine

1/4 cup packed dark brown sugar

1/2 to 1 teaspoon cinnamon

**1 loaf**
    **J. B. Dough Classic White or Whole Earth Bread**

**3 eggs**

**2 egg whites**

**1³/4 cups milk**

**¹/3 cup orange marmalade**

**¹/4 cup sugar**

**¹/2 teaspoon cinnamon**

**¹/2 teaspoon vanilla extract**

# Orange Bread Pudding

Slice bread; cut each slice into halves. Arrange in ungreased baking dish. Beat eggs, egg whites, milk, marmalade, sugar, cinnamon and vanilla in bowl. Pour over bread slices. Let stand for 15 minutes or refrigerate overnight.

Bake at 325 degrees for 35 minutes or until knife inserted in center comes out clean. Serve warm Maple-Orange Sauce over bread pudding. Makes 12 servings.

**1 tablespoon cornstarch**

**¹/4 teaspoon finely shredded orange rind**

**³/4 cup orange juice**

**¹/3 cup maple syrup**

# Maple-Orange Sauce

Mix cornstarch and orange rind in small saucepan. Stir orange juice and maple syrup into mixture of cornstarch and orange rind in saucepan. Cook until thickened, stirring constantly. Makes 1 cup.

# B r u n c h

## Carrot-Raisin Bread Pudding

Prepare bread mix following J. B. Dough package instructions. Add brown sugar with dry ingredients. Wait for the beep. Add carrots and raisins. Bake according to your manufacturer's instructions.

Slice bread into 2-inch strips. Place in greased 6x9-inch baking dish. Beat eggs, egg whites and milk in bowl. Pour over bread. Let stand for 15 minutes.

Bake at 325 degrees for 30 minutes. Sprinkle with confectioners' sugar. Serve with maple syrup. Makes 6 servings.

1 package
   J. B. Dough Whole
   Earth Bread mix

1 tablespoon brown
   sugar

1/2 cup shredded
   carrots

1/2 cup raisins

3 eggs

2 egg whites

13/4 cups milk

Confectioners' sugar

1 loaf
  J. B. Dough
  Whole Earth bread

1/2 cup chunky
  applesauce

1/4 cup chopped pecans

1/4 cup raisins
  (optional)

1/4 teaspoon cinnamon

3 eggs

11/2 cups milk

1/4 cup packed brown
  sugar

1/2 teaspoon cinnamon

1/2 teaspoon vanilla
  extract

Flour

Packed brown sugar

Margarine

# Apple Streusel Bread Pudding

Cut bread loaf into 1-inch cubes. Place 3/4 of the cubes in greased 2-quart baking dish. Combine applesauce, pecans, raisins and 1/4 teaspoon cinnamon in bowl; mix well. Spoon over bread cubes. Top with remaining cubes.

Beat eggs in medium bowl. Blend in milk, 1/4 cup brown sugar, 1/2 teaspoon cinnamon and vanilla. Pour over bread cubes. Let stand for 15 minutes. Mix flour and brown sugar in small bowl. Cut in margarine until crumbly. Sprinkle over top.

Bake at 350 degrees for 45 to 50 minutes or until knife inserted in center comes out clean. Let stand for 10 minutes before serving. Top with cream or dust with confectioners' sugar. Makes 12 servings.

# B r u n c h

## Apple-Nut Bread Pudding

Trim crust from bread. Cut loaf into cubes. Set aside to dry. Place bread cubes in ungreased 8-inch round baking dish. Melt butter in microwave-safe bowl. Add apples. Microwave on Medium for 5 minutes.

Spoon apples over bread cubes. Sprinkle with pecans. Beat eggs with milk, sugar, cinnamon and vanilla in bowl. Pour over top. Let stand for 15 minutes. Bake at 325 degrees for 35 to 40 minutes or until set. Serve with warm Caramel-Nut Sauce. Makes 8 servings.

1 loaf
  J. B. Dough
  Whole Earth Bread

2 tablespoons butter

2 medium apples,
  peeled, chopped

1/2 cup chopped pecans

4 eggs

2 1/2 cups milk

1/2 cup sugar

1/2 teaspoon cinnamon

1/2 teaspoon vanilla
  extract

## Caramel-Nut Sauce

Melt butter in small saucepan. Blend in brown sugar and corn syrup. Bring to a full rolling boil. Blend in whipping cream. Return to a full boil; remove from heat. Stir in pecans. Makes 1 cup.

1/4 cup butter

1/2 cup packed brown
  sugar

1 tablespoon light
  corn syrup

1/4 cup whipping
  cream

1/4 cup chopped pecans

# Sandwiches
# & Pizza

# Sandwiches

## Brat and Tater on Pumpernickel

Arrange sliced bread on ungreased baking sheet. Cook bratwurst and onion in skillet until onion is tender, stirring constantly; drain. Stir in potato salad. Cook for 3 minutes, stirring constantly.

Broil bread on 1 side for 3 to 5 minutes or until brown. Turn bread slices over. Spread bratwurst mixture over bread; top with cheese. Broil for 2 to 3 minutes or until cheese melts. Garnish with chives or parsley. Makes 8 servings.

1 loaf
  J. B. Dough
  Pumpernickel
  Bread, sliced

3 precooked
  bratwurst, cut into
  1/2-inch slices

1 medium onion, sliced

1   15-ounce can
  German potato salad

4 ounces Swiss cheese,
  thinly sliced

6 ground beef patties

1 loaf
   J. B. Dough
   Spicy Bread,
   cut into 12 slices or
   6 Hamburger Buns

Olive oil

1 tablespoon Dijon
   mustard

6 slices Muenster
   cheese

1 small red onion,
   sliced

## Bev's Spicy Burgers

Grill beef patties over hot coals
until cooked through. Remove to
warm platter. Brush bread slices with
olive oil. Toast on grill until brown on
both sides. Spread half the bread slices
with mustard. Top with grilled beef
patties, cheese, onion slices and lettuce.
Top with remaining bread slices.
Makes 6 servings.

1 package
   J. B. Dough
   French Bread mix

*May shape dough into
hot dog buns.*

## Hamburger Buns

Prepare bread mix following
J. B. Dough package instructions. Set
your machine on the dough mode or
on the manual setting. Remove dough
from dough machine. Divide dough
into 8 portions. Shape each portion
into 3-inch circle. Place on greased
baking sheet. Let rise in warm place
for 1 hour. Bake at 350 degrees for
20 minutes. Cool. Slice into halves.
Makes 8 servings.

# S a n d w i c h e s

## Cheese and Spinach Bruschetta

Prepare bread mix following J. B. Dough package instructions. Set your machine on the dough mode or on the manual setting.

Remove dough from bread machine. Shape into long roll. Place on greased baking sheet or in French loaf pan. Cut 3 diagonal slashes with sharp knife; brush with mixture of egg and water. Let rise in warm place for 1 hour.

Bake at 350 degrees for 25 to 30 minutes or until brown. Remove to wire rack to cool completely. Slice loaf into halves lengthwise. Place cut side up on ungreased baking sheet. Drizzle with mixture of olive oil and garlic.

Squeeze moisture from spinach. Spoon mixture of spinach and Parmesan cheese over bread halves; sprinkle with Italian seasoning, fennel seeds and basil. Top with chopped tomato and mozzarella cheese. Bake at 350 degrees for 7 to 9 minutes or until cheese melts and edges of bread are brown. Makes 15 servings.

1 package
J. B. Dough
Vienna Bread mix

1 egg, beaten

2 teaspoons water

3 tablespoons olive oil

1 clove of garlic, finely chopped

1   10-ounce package frozen spinach, cooked, drained

1 tablespoon grated Parmesan cheese

1 teaspoon Italian seasoning

1/2 teaspoon fennel seeds

1/2 teaspoon basil

1 tomato, seeds removed, chopped

6 ounces mozzarella cheese, sliced

1 package
   J. B. Dough
   Vienna Bread mix

1 egg, beaten

2 teaspoons water

1 medium onion,
   thinly sliced

1 large green onion,
   thinly sliced

1 clove of garlic, finely
   chopped

2 tablespoons olive oil

1 envelope au jus
   gravy mix

Fresh au jus to taste

8 ounces Chicago
   roast beef, thinly

*You can buy fresh au jus
at your favorite deli.*

# Chicago-Style French Dip Sandwiches

Prepare bread mix following
J. B. Dough package instructions. Set
your machine on the dough mode or
on the manual setting.

Remove dough from bread machine.
Divide dough into 2 portions. Shape
into 2 baguettes. Place on baking
sheet. Cut 3 diagonal slashes with
sharp knife; brush with mixture of
egg and water. Let rise in warm
place for 1 hour.

Bake at 350 degrees for 25 minutes.
Remove to wire rack to cool
completely. Cut loaves into halves
lengthwise; cut into thirds.

Sauté onion, green onion and garlic
in olive oil in skillet until onions are
tender. Prepare gravy mix in skillet
using package directions. Stir in fresh
au jus. Add roast beef. Cook just
until heated through.

Place sliced bread on plate. Drizzle
with 2 tablespoons gravy. Top with
roast beef and onion mixture. Cover
sandwich with remaining bread.
Serve with potato salad and sliced
tomato. Makes 6 servings.

# Sandwiches

## Layered Club Sandwiches

Prepare bread mix following J. B. Dough package instructions. Set your machine on the dough mode or on the manual setting.

Remove dough from bread machine. Shape into round loaf. Place in greased 10-inch round bread pan. Brush with mixture of egg and water. Let rise in warm place for 1 hour.

Bake at 350 degrees for 25 to 30 minutes. Remove to wire rack to cool completely. Slice top from bread 1/3 down; remove center carefully, leaving shell. Spread Italian dressing on bread top and inside bread shell.

Layer cheese, roast beef, turkey, tomato, red onion and lettuce 1/2 at a time in shell. Replace bread top; cut into wedges. Serve with pasta salad for a great luncheon treat. Makes 8 servings.

1 package
    J. B. Dough
    Vienna Bread mix

1 egg, beaten

2 teaspoons water

3/4 cup creamy Italian
    salad dressing

8 ounces Swiss cheese,
    thinly sliced

8 ounces deli-style
    roast beef, thinly
    sliced

8 ounces deli-style
    turkey, thinly sliced

1 large tomato, sliced

1 small red onion,
    thinly sliced

Lettuce leaves

*Use bread removed from center of loaf for bread crumbs.*

2 loaves
   J. B. Dough
   Vienna Bread

2 cloves of garlic,
   crushed

1/4 cup Dijon mustard

12 ounces honey
   baked ham, thinly
   sliced

12 ounces roast pork,
   thinly sliced

4 dill pickles, thinly
   sliced

8 ounces baby Swiss
   cheese, thinly sliced

2 tablespoons oil

# Hot Cuban Sandwiches

Slice loaves into halves lengthwise. Brush cut side of bread with crushed garlic; spread with Dijon mustard. Layer ham, pork, dill pickles and Swiss cheese over bread; top with remaining bread. Sauté each sandwich in 1 tablespoon oil in skillet until the cheese melts and bread is golden brown. Serve with a large Caesar salad. Makes 2 sandwich loaves.

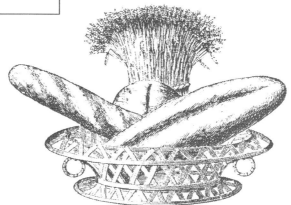

# Sandwiches

## Spicy Ham and Cheese Melt

Place bread slices on baking sheet. Toast under broiler until brown on both sides. Spread bread slices with mixture of butter, Dijon mustard and poppy seeds. Arrange ham slices and cheese slices over butter mixture on half the bread slices; top with remaining bread slices.

Wrap each sandwich in foil. Place on baking sheet. Bake at 350 degrees for 15 to 20 minutes or until heated through. Makes 6 sandwiches.

1 loaf
   J. B. Dough
   Spicy Bread,
   cut into 12 slices

2 tablespoons butter,
   softened

2 teaspoons Dijon
   mustard

$1/2$ teaspoon poppy
   seeds

6 slices boiled ham

6 slices Swiss cheese or
   any variety of cheese

*Great to take to football games.*

*To keep sandwiches warm, heat a brick or tile in oven with sandwiches. Arrange folded newspapers in canvas bag; place hot brick or tile between newspapers. Place hot sandwiches on top of newspapers; cover with towel. Top with more newspapers. The sandwiches will stay warm for hours on a cold day.*

1 package
  J. B. Dough
  Onion Dill
  Bread mix

1 teaspoon Italian
  seasoning

2   9-ounce jars
  marinated
  artichoke hearts

8 ounces prosciutto,
  thinly sliced

8 ounces salami, thinly
  sliced

8 ounces provolone
  cheese, thinly sliced

1 small red onion,
  thinly sliced

*Delicious for football
games or picnics.*

# Italian Sandwich Loaf

Prepare bread mix following
J. B. Dough package instructions. Add
Italian seasoning with dry ingredients.
Set your machine on the dough mode
or on the manual setting.

Remove dough from bread machine.
Shape into round loaf. Place in
greased 10-inch round bread pan.
Let rise in warm place for 1 hour.

Bake at 350 degrees for 25 to 30
minutes or until brown. Remove to
wire rack to cool completely. Slice
top from loaf 1/3 down. Cut loaf into
halves lengthwise. Drain artichokes,
reserving marinade.

Drizzle 1/2 of the reserved marinade
over top and bottom of loaf. Layer
prosciutto, salami, cheese, onion,
artichokes and remaining marinade
1/2 at a time over bottom of bread.
Top with bread top, pressing lightly;
secure with wooden picks. Store in
refrigerator for 2 to 3 hours if
desired. Cut into wedges.
Makes 8 wedges.

# S a n d w i c h e s

## Muffaletta

Prepare bread mix following J. B. Dough package instructions. Add 1 tablespoon olive oil with liquid ingredients. Set your machine on the dough mode or on the manual setting.

Remove dough from bread machine. Shape into round loaf. Place in greased 10-inch round bread pan or on a baking sheet. Cut slashes with sharp knife. Let rise in warm place for 1 hour.

Bake at 350 degrees for 25 to 30 minutes or until brown. Remove to wire rack to cool completely. Drain artichoke hearts, reserving 2 tablespoons marinade. Slice loaf horizontally 1/3 down from top; remove some of center carefully. Brush inside of loaf with olive oil; spread with Dijon mustard. Layer ham, turkey, cheese, onion, olives, feta cheese and artichokes in bread shell. Drizzle with reserved marinade; top with shredded lettuce. Replace bread top, pressing gently. Cut into wedges. Makes 8 wedges.

1 package
J. B. Dough
Vienna Bread mix

1 tablespoon olive oil

1  9-ounce jar
marinated artichoke
hearts

Olive oil to taste

Dijon mustard to taste

8 ounces honey-baked
ham, thinly sliced

8 ounces smoked
turkey, thinly sliced

8 ounces baby Swiss
cheese, thinly sliced

1 small red onion,
thinly sliced

Italian olives or black
olives, sliced

3 ounces feta cheese,
crumbled

Shredded lettuce

*Wrap in plastic wrap and store in refrigerator until serving time.*

*Good for the beach and picnics because it holds so well.*

1 package
  J. B. Dough
  Vienna Bread mix

4 onions, sliced

1/2 teaspoon salt

Pepper to taste

1 tablespoon canola oil

16 ounces frozen thin
  sandwich steaks,
  thawed

3 tablespoons canola
  oil

8 slices American
  cheese

# Philadelphia Cheese-Steak Sandwiches

Prepare bread mix following
J. B. Dough package instructions. Set
your machine on the dough mode or
on the manual setting.

Remove dough from bread machine.
Divide into 4 portions. Shape into
4 rolls. Place on greased baking sheet.
Let rise in warm place for 1 hour.

Bake at 350 degrees for 25 to 30
minutes or until brown. Remove to
wire rack to cool completely. Slice
lengthwise into halves.

Sauté onions, salt and pepper in
1 tablespoon oil in skillet until
onions are tender and brown.
Remove onions. Fry steaks in small
batches in 1 tablespoon oil in same
skillet until of desired degree of
doneness; push to side. Brush
cut side of rolls with remaining
2 tablespoons canola oil. Cook rolls
in skillet cut side down until crisp
and brown. Place rolls on serving
platter. Layer steaks, cheese and
onions on bottoms of rolls; replace
bread tops. Makes 4 sandwiches.

# Sandwiches

## Torpedo Sandwiches

Prepare bread mix following J. B. Dough package instructions. Set your machine on the dough mode or on the manual setting.

Remove dough from bread machine. Divide dough into 4 portions. Shape into 4 rolls. Place on greased baking sheet. Let rise in warm place for 1 hour.

Bake at 350 degrees for 25 to 30 minutes or until brown. Remove to wire rack to cool completely. Slice horizontally into halves. Spread cut sides of bread with mayonnaise and mustard; sprinkle with pepper. Layer bologna, salami, Cheddar cheese, Swiss cheese, tomato slices and lettuce on half the rolls; top with remaining halves. Makes 4 sandwiches.

1 package
  J. B. Dough
  Vienna Bread mix

1/2 cup mayonnaise

1 tablespoon prepared
  mustard

Pepper to taste

6 ounces bologna,
  thinly sliced

6 ounces salami, thinly
  sliced

4 ounces Cheddar
  cheese, thinly sliced

4 ounces Swiss cheese,
  thinly sliced

2 tomatoes, sliced

4 lettuce leaves

*May substitute any of your favorite lunch meats and cheeses.*

*To take sandwiches to the beach, wrap sandwiches in plastic wrap and store in cooler. Wrap lettuce separately; place on sandwiches just before serving.*

1 package
   J. B. Dough
   California Sour
   Dough Bread mix

6 ounces deli-style
   turkey, thinly sliced

1/4 cup pesto

1 medium tomato,
   sliced

1 small zucchini,
   thinly sliced

8 thin slices mozzarella
   or Muenster cheese

*Sandwich is easy to
assemble and bake
when you have been out
boating. It's filling for
those tired sailors.*

## Grilled Turkey on Sour Dough Loaf

Prepare bread mix following
J. B. Dough package instructions.
Set your machine on the dough mode
or on the manual setting.

Remove dough from bread machine.
Shape into round loaf. Place in
greased 10-inch round bread pan
or on baking sheet. Let rise in warm
place for 1 hour.

Bake at 350 degrees for 25 to 30
minutes or until brown. Remove to
wire rack to cool completely. Slice
loaf horizontally 1 inch from top;
remove center carefully, leaving shell.

Layer turkey, pesto, tomato, zucchini
and cheese 1/2 at a time in shell;
replace bread top. Wrap in foil.
Place on baking sheet. Bake at 350
degrees for 25 to 30 minutes or heat
on grill for 40 minutes; cut into
wedges. Serve with sliced tomatoes
and mozzarella cheese drizzled with
Italian dressing. Makes 8 wedges.

# P i z z a

## Mini Bacon-Onion Pizzas

Prepare bread mix following J. B. Dough package instructions. Add olive oil with liquid ingredients. Set your machine on the dough mode or on the manual setting.

Remove dough from bread machine. Divide dough into 4 portions. Shape each portion into round circle. Place on greased baking sheet; sprinkle with cheese. Top with mixture of bacon, green pepper, red onion, green onions and chives. Bake at 375 degrees for 15 to 20 minutes or until cheese melts. Makes 4 mini pizzas.

1 package
  J. B. Dough
  Vienna Bread mix

1 tablespoon olive oil

4 ounces provolone
  cheese, shredded

4 slices Canadian
  bacon, chopped

$1/2$ green bell pepper,
  chopped

1 small red onion,
  chopped

4 green onions, finely
  chopped

1 tablespoon chopped
  chives

1 package
  J. B. Dough
  Vienna Bread mix

1 tablespoon olive oil

8 ounces ground beef

1 small red onion,
  chopped

Olive oil

8 ounces shredded
  Cheddar cheese

## Cheeseburger Mini Pizzas

Prepare bread mix following J. B. Dough package instructions. Add 1 tablespoon olive oil with liquid ingredients. Set your machine on the dough mode or on the manual setting.

Remove dough from bread machine. Divide dough into 4 portions. Shape into 4 circles. Place on greased baking sheet.

Brown ground beef with onion in skillet, stirring until ground beef is crumbly; drain. Brush each dough circle with olive oil. Spread ground beef mixture over top; sprinkle with cheese. Bake at 375 degrees for 15 to 20 minutes or until cheese melts. Makes 4 mini pizzas.

# Pizza

## Stir-Fried Chicken Pizza

Prepare bread mix following J. B. Dough package instructions. Add 1 tablespoon olive oil with liquid ingredients. Set your machine on the dough mode or on the manual setting.

Remove dough from bread machine. Roll into large circle on lightly floured surface. Place in greased pizza pan. Bake at 350 degrees for 10 minutes.

Brush baked layer with olive oil. Combine green pepper, onion, mushrooms, 1 tablespoon olive oil and butter in microwave-safe dish. Microwave for 3 minutes; drain. Arrange chicken strips and vegetable mixture over baked layer; sprinkle with cheeses. Bake for 10 minutes. Brush crust with additional olive oil. Makes 8 servings.

1 package
    J. B. Dough
    Vienna Bread mix

1 tablespoon olive oil

Olive oil

1 green bell pepper,
    cut into strips

1 medium onion, cut
    into strips

1   4-ounce can sliced
    mushrooms, drained

1 tablespoon olive oil

1 tablespoon butter

2 chicken breast filets,
    cooked, cut into
    strips

1/2 cup shredded
    Monterey Jack
    cheese

1/2 cup shredded
    mozzarella cheese

# P i z z a

8 ounces Italian
  sausage, sliced

1 loaf
  J. B. Dough
  Vienna Bread

Olive oil

1  15-ounce jar pizza
  sauce

3 ounces pepperoni,
  thinly sliced

3 tablespoons chopped
  green onions

Sliced black olives

Sliced mushrooms

1 cup shredded
  mozzarella cheese

2 tablespoons grated
  Parmesan cheese

Garlic powder to taste

Italian seasoning to
  taste

## Easy Pizza

Microwave sausage in microwave-safe dish for 2 to 3 minutes or until sausage is no longer pink; drain. Slice bread into halves horizontally. Brush cut sides of bread lightly with olive oil. Place cut side up on ungreased baking sheet. Bake at 350 degrees until light brown.

Spread pizza sauce over bread. Layer sausage, pepperoni, green onions, black olives, mushrooms, mozzarella cheese and Parmesan cheese in order listed over sauce. Sprinkle with garlic powder and Italian seasoning. Bake for 12 to 15 minutes or until cheese melts. Cut into wedges. Serve with your favorite salad. Makes 8 servings.

# P i z z a

## Garlic and Cheese Pizza

Prepare bread mix following J. B. Dough package instructions. Add 1 tablespoon olive oil with liquid ingredients. Set your machine on the dough mode or on the manual setting.

Remove dough from machine. Roll into a circle on lightly floured surface. Place in greased pizza pan. Brush with additional olive oil. Bake at 350 degrees for 10 minutes. Spread baked layer with mayonnaise; sprinkle with Parmesan cheese, red onion, basil and garlic. Bake for 10 minutes. Cut into wedges. Makes 8 servings.

| |
| --- |
| 1 package J. B. Dough Vienna Bread mix |
| Olive oil |
| 1/2 cup mayonnaise |
| 1/2 cup grated Parmesan cheese |
| 1 small red onion, thinly sliced |
| 1/4 cup fresh basil strips |
| 3 cloves of garlic, finely chopped |

1 package
    J. B. Dough
    Country Rye
    Bread mix

1 tablespoon olive oil

$^1/_3$ cup mayonnaise

2 teaspoons
    horseradish sauce

1 teaspoon prepared
    mustard

1 tablespoon chopped
    chives

8 ounces ham,
    shredded

1   4-ounce can sliced
    mushrooms, drained
    (optional)

6 ounces Swiss cheese,
    shredded

Olive oil

*May cut into small
pieces and serve as an
appetizer.*

## Ham and Swiss Rye Pizza

Prepare bread mix following
J. B. Dough package instructions. Add
1 tablespoon olive oil with liquid
ingredients. Set your machine on the
dough mode or on the manual setting.

Remove dough from machine. Roll
into a circle on lightly floured
surface. Place in greased pizza pan.
Bake at 350 degrees for 10 minutes.

Spread baked layer with mayonnaise,
horseradish sauce and mustard.
Sprinkle with chives, ham and
mushrooms; top with cheese. Bake
for 9 to 10 minutes or until cheese
melts. Brush edge of pizza with olive
oil; cut into wedges. Makes 8 servings.

# P i z z a

## Rosemary-Garlic Focaccia

Prepare bread mix following J. B. Dough package instructions. Add 1 tablespoon olive oil with liquid ingredients. Set your machine on the dough mode or on the manual setting.

Remove dough from bread machine. Roll into a circle on lightly floured surface. Place in greased 12-inch pizza pan or 9x13-inch baking pan. Let rise in warm place for 30 minutes. Pierce holes 1 inch apart in dough with wooden spoon handle. Brush with mixture of garlic, rosemary, egg white and 2 tablespoons olive oil. Bake at 350 degrees for 15 to 20 minutes or until heated through. Cut into wedges. Makes 8 servings.

1 package
J. B. Dough
Classic White
Bread mix

3 tablespoons olive oil

2 cloves of garlic,
finely chopped

1 tablespoon chopped
fresh rosemary or
1 teaspoon dried
rosemary

1 egg white, beaten

1 package
  J. B. Dough
  Vienna Bread mix

2 tablespoons olive oil

1/4 cup reduced-calorie
  mayonnaise

16 ounces Monterey
  Jack cheese or
  Muenster cheese,
  thinly sliced

8 ounces deli-style
  turkey breast, thinly
  sliced

8 ounces boiled ham,
  thinly sliced

1 small tomato, seeds
  removed, cut into
  strips

2 tablespoons fresh
  basil strips

1 tablespoon chopped
  fresh chives

3 ounces Swiss cheese,
  thinly sliced

## Easy Turkey Club Pizza

Prepare bread mix following
J. B. Dough package instructions. Add
1 tablespoon olive oil with liquid
ingredients. Set your machine on the
dough mode or on the manual setting.

Remove dough from bread machine.
Roll into a circle on lightly floured
surface. Place in greased pizza pan.
Bake at 350 degrees for 10 minutes.

Brush baked layer with 1 tablespoon
olive oil; spread with mayonnaise.
Stack Monterey Jack cheese, turkey
and ham; cut into small strips.
Arrange strips over mayonnaise;
sprinkle with tomato, basil and
chives. Top with Swiss cheese. Bake
at 350 degrees for 10 minutes. Cut
into wedges. Makes 8 servings.

# Pizza

## Veggie Pizza

Prepare bread mix following
J. B. Dough package instructions.
Add olive oil with liquid ingredients.
Set your machine on the dough mode
or on the manual setting.

Remove dough from bread machine.
Roll into a 12-inch circle on lightly
floured surface. Place in greased pizza
pan. Bake at 350 degrees
for 10 minutes.

Combine zucchini, yellow squash,
green or red pepper, garlic, onion,
sundried tomatoes and 1 tablespoon
oil in microwave-safe dish.
Microwave on High for 6 minutes
or until vegetables are tender,
stirring twice.

Spread pizza sauce over baked layer;
top with vegetable mixture. Sprinkle
with mozzarella cheese, Parmesan
cheese, chives and basil. Bake for 10
minutes or until cheese melts. Cut
into wedges. Makes 8 servings.

1 package
 J. B. Dough
 Vienna Bread mix

1 tablespoon olive oil

1 small zucchini,
 chopped

1 small yellow squash,
 chopped

1 green or red bell
 pepper, cut into
 julienne strips

1 clove of garlic, finely
 chopped

1 small onion, thinly
 sliced

1/2 cup oil-pack
 sundried tomato
 strips

1 tablespoon oil

1   6-ounce jar
 mushroom pizza
 sauce

1 cup shredded
 mozzarella cheese

1/3 cup grated
 Parmesan cheese

Chopped fresh chives
 and basil to taste

1 package
  J. B. Dough
  Vienna Bread mix

2 tablespoons olive oil

1 cup black olives

2 teaspoons red wine
  vinegar

1 teaspoon drained
  capers

1 teaspoon olive oil

2 cloves of garlic,
  chopped

1 cup chopped red or
  yellow tomatoes

2 tablespoons finely
  chopped green
  onions

1 tablespoon olive oil

1 teaspoon dried basil
  or 1 tablespoon
  chopped fresh basil

1 teaspoon parsley
  flakes or 1
  tablespoon fresh
  chopped parsley

Freshly ground pepper

1/2 cup grated fresh
  Parmesan cheese

*May store olive mixture
in refrigerator for 2 days.*

## Easy Bruschetta Appetizers

Prepare bread mix following
J. B. Dough package instructions. Set
your machine on the dough mode
or on the manual setting.

Remove dough from bread machine.
Shape dough into 2 baguettes. Place
on greased baking sheet or in double
baguette pan. Let rise in warm place
for 1 hour. Bake at 350 degrees for
25 to 30 minutes or until brown.

Remove to wire rack to cool. Cut
loaves into 1/2-inch slices. Brush on
both sides with 2 tablespoons olive
oil. Place on ungreased baking sheet.
Bake at 425 degrees for 5 minutes or
until light brown on both sides,
turning once. Cool.

Purée olives, wine vinegar, capers,
1 teaspoon olive oil and garlic in food
processor. Combine tomatoes, green
onions, 1 tablespoon olive oil, basil,
parsley and pepper in bowl. Spread
bread slices with thin layer of olive
mixture. Top with 2 tablespoons
tomato mixture; sprinkle with
Parmesan cheese. Place on baking
sheet. Bake for 2 to 3 minutes or just
until cheese melts. Serve warm.
Makes 24 servings.

# Pizza

## Calzones

Prepare bread mix following J. B. Dough package instructions. Add olive oil with liquid ingredients. Set your machine on the dough mode or on the manual setting.

Remove dough from bread machine. Divide dough into 2 portions. Roll into two 9-inch circles on lightly floured surface. Arrange mozzarella cheese and prosciutto on circles; sprinkle with chives, garlic powder, Italian seasoning and basil. Moisten edges of dough with water. Fold over to enclose filling, sealing edge. Place on lightly greased baking sheet.

Let rise in warm place for 45 minutes. Cut diagonal slash in top of each with sharp knife; brush with mixture of egg and water. Sprinkle with Parmesan cheese. Bake at 350 degrees for 25 to 30 minutes. Serve warm. Makes 2 calzones.

1 package J. B. Dough Classic White Bread mix

1 tablespoon olive oil

12 ounces shredded mozzarella cheese

3 ounces prosciutto or ham, cut into strips

3 tablespoons chopped chives

1/2 teaspoon garlic powder

1/2 teaspoon Italian seasoning

1/4 teaspoon basil

1 egg, beaten

2 teaspoons water

2 tablespoons grated Parmesan cheese

1 package
J. B. Dough
Classic White
Bread mix

3/4 cup tomato sauce

1 teaspoon Italian
seasoning

1/2 teaspoon garlic salt

2 tablespoons finely
chopped green
onions

2 tablespoons finely
sliced black olives

12 slices pepperoni

1 cup shredded
mozzarella cheese

1/3 cup grated
Parmesan cheese

## Pizza Muffins

Prepare bread mix following
J. B. Dough package instructions. Set
your machine on the dough mode or
on the manual setting.

Remove dough from bread machine.
Divide dough into 12 portions. Pat
each portion into a circle; press into
greased muffin cup. Spoon mixture
of tomato sauce, Italian seasoning
and garlic salt into each muffin
cup. Top with green onions, black
olives and pepperoni. Sprinkle with
mozzarella cheese and Parmesan
cheese. Bake at 400 degrees for 12
to 15 minutes or until brown.
Makes 12 servings.

# Pizza

## Stuffed Pizza Roll

Prepare bread mix following J. B. Dough package instructions. Set your machine on the dough mode or on the manual setting.

Remove dough from bread machine. Roll into rectangle on lightly floured surface.

Brown ground beef with onion in skillet, stirring until ground beef is crumbly; drain. Spread pizza sauce over dough to within 1 inch of edge. Spoon ground beef mixture over sauce; sprinkle with Italian seasoning and garlic powder. Top with mozzarella cheese and Parmesan cheese. Roll as for jelly roll to enclose filling, sealing edge.

Place seam side down on ungreased baking sheet. Cut 3 slashes in top with sharp knife; brush with mixture of egg and water. Let rise in warm place for 1 hour. Bake at 350 degrees for 25 to 30 minutes. Serve with a salad. Makes 8 servings.

1 package J. B. Dough Vienna Bread mix

8 ounces ground beef

1 small onion, chopped

1 15-ounce jar pizza sauce

1/2 teaspoon Italian seasoning

1/2 teaspoon garlic powder

8 ounces mozzarella cheese, shredded

2 tablespoons grated Parmesan cheese

1 egg, beaten

2 teaspoons water

# *Holiday*

# H o l i d a y

## Mom's Teddy Bear

Prepare bread mix following J. B. Dough package instructions. Add honey with liquid. Add almonds if desired. Set your machine on the dough mode or on the manual setting. Remove dough from bread machine. Divide dough into 2 equal portions on lightly floured surface.

Shape 1 portion into a ball; place on greased baking sheet. Divide remaining dough into 2 portions. Shape 1 portion into a ball; position on baking sheet for head. Divide remaining dough into 5 pieces. Shape 4 of the pieces for hands and feet, flattening slightly and snipping with scissors to make fingers and toes. Position on baking sheet, pressing hands, feet and head to connect firmly with body. Divide remaining dough into 3 pieces; flatten slightly. Position ears and nose on head; press firmly. Press 2 raisins into head to make eyes, 1 raisin for the nose and remaining raisin into body for belly button.

Brush with mixture of egg and water. Sprinkle with Vanilla Sugar. Let rise in warm place for 1 hour or until doubled in bulk. Bake at 350 degrees for 25 to 30 minutes or until golden. Makes 1 Teddy Bear.

1 package
  J. B. Dough
  Whole Earth
  Bread mix

1 tablespoon honey

1/4 cup slivered
  almonds (optional)

4 raisins

1 egg, beaten

2 teaspoons water

Vanilla Sugar
  (page 89)

*Tie thin red ribbon around Teddy Bear neck for giving. Teddy Bear makes a great gift for parents of newborn baby. Place in a basket with a jar of Honey Butter (page 17) and a baby gift. The parents will be delighted.*

| |
|---|
| 1 vanilla bean |
| 1 quart jar |
| Sugar |

## Vanilla Sugar

Place vanilla bean in clean quart jar. Fill jar to the top with sugar. Place jar lid on tightly. Place in dark warm place for 3 weeks.

# Holiday

## Christmas Candy Cane Bread

Prepare bread mix following J. B. Dough package instructions. Set your machine on the dough mode or on the manual setting.

Remove dough from bread machine. Roll dough into 15x18-inch rectangle on lightly floured surface. Place chopped cherries, apricots and 3 tablespoons slivered almonds lengthwise down center.

Make 2-inch cuts at $1/2$-inch intervals on long sides of rectangle. Fold strips diagonally across filling; stretch and shape to form cane. Place on greased baking sheet. Let rise in warm place for 1 hour. Brush with mixture of egg and water.

Bake at 350 degrees for 25 to 30 minutes or until brown. Remove to wire rack to cool completely. Blend confectioners' sugar and milk in small bowl. Drizzle over cooled bread. Decorate with whole candied cherries and almond slivers. Makes 1 Candy Cane Bread.

1 package
   J. B. Dough
   Sweet Bread mix

3 tablespoons finely chopped candied cherries

3 tablespoons finely chopped dried apricots

3 tablespoons slivered almonds

1 egg, beaten

2 teaspoons water

$1/2$ cup confectioners' sugar

4 teaspoons milk

Candied cherries

Almond slivers

*Wrap with plastic wrap and a large red bow. Great Christmas gift.*

1 package
 J. B. Dough
 Sweet Bread mix

2 teaspoons grated
 lemon rind

3 tablespoons melted
 butter or margarine

1/4 cup raisins

1/4 cup walnuts

3 tablespoons brown
 sugar

2 teaspoons grated
 orange rind

1 teaspoon grated
 lemon rind

1/2 teaspoon cinnamon

3 tablespoons chopped
 dried apricots

1 egg, beaten

2 teaspoons water

Confectioners' sugar

## Christmas Wreath

Prepare bread mix following
J. B. Dough package instructions.
Add 2 teaspoons lemon rind to mix.
Set your machine on the dough mode
or on the manual setting.

Remove dough from bread machine.
Roll dough to 15x18-inch rectangle
on lightly floured surface. Cut long
strip from dough and reserve.

Spread remaining dough with butter
to within 1 inch of edge. Sprinkle
with raisins, walnuts, brown sugar,
orange rind and 1 teaspoon lemon
rind, cinnamon and apricots. Roll as
for jelly roll; pinch seam to seal.

Shape into circle around empty
4-inch can on greased baking sheet;
seal ends together. Let rise in warm
place for 1 hour.

Roll reserved dough to 1/8-inch
thickness; cut into desired shapes
such as holly leaves, hearts or stars.
Moisten cutouts with a small amount
of water; attach to wreath as desired.
Brush wreath and cutouts with
mixture of egg and 2 teaspoons water.
Bake at 350 degrees for 25 to 30
minutes or until golden brown.
Sprinkle with confectioners' sugar.
Makes 1 Christmas Wreath.

## Christmas Bow Wreath

1 package
J. B. Dough
Vienna Bread mix

Baking parchment

1 egg, beaten

2 teaspoons water

Sesame seeds

Prepare bread mix following J. B. Dough package instructions. Set your machine on the dough mode or on the manual setting.

Remove dough from bread machine. Divide dough into 16 equal pieces. Shape each piece into 6 to 8-inch long rope on lightly floured surface. Handle dough gently or bread will be tough. Tie each rope loosely into knot. Grease baking parchment; place on baking sheet.

Arrange knots in circle on parchment. Be sure that all knots face the same direction. Brush with mixture of egg and water; sprinkle with sesame seeds. Let rise in warm place for 1 hour. Bake at 350 degrees for 20 to 25 minutes or until light brown. Place wreath on serving plate. Place large red bow at top of wreath if desired. Serve warm as dinner rolls with your favorite flavored butter. Makes 16 servings.

*Decorate any bread wreath with a large red bow for a festive presentation.*

## Pumpernickel-Cheese Wreath

1 package
   J. B. Dough
   Pumpernickel
   Bread mix

1 egg

2 teaspoons water

1   8-ounce round brie
   or your favorite
   cheese

1/4 cup sliced almonds

*Serve with a dark beer
while watching a good
football game.*

Prepare bread mix following
J. B. Dough package instructions. Set
your machine on the dough mode or
on the manual setting.

Remove dough from bread machine.
Divide dough into 2 portions on
lightly floured surface. Shape each
into long rope. Grease outside of
10-ounce custard cup; place on
greased baking sheet. Twist dough
ropes together gently; shape into
ring around custard cup and seal
ends together.

Brush with mixture of egg and water;
reserve remaining egg wash. Let rise
in warm place for 1 hour. Bake at 350
degrees for 25 minutes. Remove
custard cup. Cool wreath on baking
sheet on wire rack.

Place brie in center of wreath. Brush
with reserved egg wash; sprinkle with
almonds. Place under preheated
broiler for several minutes to soften
brie and toast almonds. Serve
warm. Makes 1 Pumpernickel-
Cheese Wreath.

## Date and Almond Stollen

Mix bread mix dry ingredients, 1 table-spoon brown sugar and lemon rind together. Beat egg in 1-cup measure. Add enough warm water to measure 200 cc or 7/8 cup. Pour into bread machine. Add bread mix. Set your machine on the dough mode or on the manual setting. Wait for beep; add slivered almonds. Remove dough from bread machine.

Roll to 1/2-inch thickness on lightly floured surface. Spread with Date Filling. Roll as for jelly roll from opposite sides to meet in center; press to flatten in center.

Place on greased baking sheet. Let rise in warm place for 45 minutes. Bake at 350 degrees for 25 to 30 minutes or until golden brown. Remove to wire rack to cool.

Combine egg white, confectioners' sugar and lemon juice in mixing bowl, stirring until of spreading consistency. Frost stollen while slightly warm; sprinkle with sliced almonds. Makes 1 Date and Almond Stollen.

1 package
  J. B. Dough
  Classic White
  Bread mix

1 tablespoon brown
  sugar

1 teaspoon grated
  lemon rind

1 egg, at room
  temperature

1/4 cup slivered
  almonds

Date Filling (page 95)

1 egg white

3/4 cup confectioners'
  sugar

1 teaspoon lemon juice

3 tablespoons sliced
  almonds

## Gift Basket Idea or New House Gift

*Make up a basket for a housewarming gift or for the first time you visit someone's home. Fill the basket with salt, wine and either fresh bread or a package of pre-mix for them to bake themselves or put in both. You may put in other things as well, such as a bread knife, cookbook, jams and jellies or just let your imagination go. It's my favorite gift to give, a tradition which started as a wedding gift to John and me.*

*Include a favorite saying. Mine, a special good luck one, comes from one of my favorite Christmas movies,* **It's a Wonderful Life.**

**Salt: may life always have flavor.
Wine: joy and prosperity forever.
Bread: this house may never know hunger.**

## Date Filling

2 tablespoons cornstarch
1 cup milk
1 egg yolk
3 tablespoons sugar
$^1/_2$ cup chopped dates
1 tablespoon butter

Blend cornstarch with a small amount of milk in bowl. Mix in egg yolk and sugar. Combine dates and remaining milk in small saucepan. Bring to a boil, stirring constantly. Stir a small amount of hot mixture into egg mixture; stir egg mixture into hot mixture. Bring to a boil, stirring constantly. Cook until thickened, stirring constantly. Stir in butter. Let stand until cool, stirring frequently to prevent skin from forming on top.

# H o l i d a y

## Christmas Stollen

Combine egg, rum and vanilla in 1 cup measure. Add enough warm water to measure 200 cc or 7/8 cup. Pour into bread machine. Add bread mix dry ingredients. Prepare bread following J. B. Dough package instructions.

Set your machine on the dough mode or on the manual setting. Wait for the beep. Add raisins, almonds, candied lemon and orange peel and dried lemon peel. Remove dough at dough mode. Divide into 3 equal portions on lightly floured surface.

Roll each into 12-inch long oval that is thinner in center than at edges. Fold dough over end to end to make 6-inch length. Arrange 2 on greased baking sheet; place the third on top in middle.

Let rise in warm place for 1 hour. Bake at 350 degrees for 25 to 30 minutes. Spread warm loaf with melted butter; sprinkle generously with confectioners' sugar. Makes 1 Christmas Stollen.

1 package
J. B. Dough
Sweet Bread mix

1 egg, beaten

1 tablespoon rum

1/2 teaspoon vanilla
extract

1/4 cup raisins

1/4 cup slivered
almonds

2 tablespoons chopped
candied lemon peel

2 tablespoons chopped
candied orange peel

1 teaspoon dried
lemon peel

Melted butter

Confectioners' sugar

1 loaf
  J. B. Dough
  French Bread

1 small orange

2 cups fresh cranberries

1 1/2 cups sugar

1/2 teaspoon almond
  extract

3 eggs

1 1/2 cups milk

1/2 cup cream

1/4 cup flour

Confectioners' sugar

Crème fraîche

*We have this on
Thanksgiving morning;
it is a great beginning
to a special day. All the
work is done the night
before and it bakes
while you stuff the
turkey. Serve with your
favorite breakfast
sausage and fresh orange
juice. It will warm up
the kitchen and brings
everyone into the
kitchen to help!*

# Cranberry Bread Pudding

Trim crust from bread loaf; reserve for another purpose. Cut loaf into 8 slices; cut slices into halves diagonally. Arrange half the slices in greased 2-quart square baking pan.Cut zest from orange; set aside. Remove and discard white pith from orange. Slice orange and discard seeds. Combine orange slices, orange zest and cranberries in food processor container. Process just until coarsely chopped. Add 1/2 cup sugar and almond extract; pulse several times to mix.

Beat eggs with milk, cream, flour and remaining 1 cup sugar in medium bowl. Spread bread in baking dish with cranberry mixture. Add half the egg mixture. Top with remaining bread slices and remaining egg mixture.

Refrigerate, covered with plastic wrap, overnight. Bake at 325 degrees for 50 to 60 minutes or until knife inserted in center comes out clean. Dust with confectioners' sugar. Serve with crème fraîche. Makes 6 to 8 servings.

# Holiday

## Aunt Ella's Fruit Loaf

Prepare bread mix with warm water, lemon juice, lemon rind, 2 teaspoons Vanilla Sugar and cardamom following J. B. Dough package instructions. Set your machine on the dough mode or on the manual setting. If your machine has light or sweet mode use that setting.

At the first beep add raisins, almonds and candied lemon peel. Remove dough from bread machine. Form into desired shape such as round, ring or standard loaf. Place in greased baking pan. Let rise in warm place for 1 hour.

Brush with mixture of egg and 2 teaspoons water. Bake at 350 degrees for 30 minutes. Cool on wire rack. Dust with confectioners' sugar. Makes 1 Fruit Loaf.

1 package
  J. B. Dough
  Classic White
  Bread mix

150 cc warm water

50 cc lemon juice

1 teaspoon grated
  dried or fresh
  lemon rind

2 teaspoons Vanilla
  Sugar (page 89)

1 teaspoon cardamom

1/4 cup raisins

2 tablespoons slivered
  almonds

2 tablespoons candied
  lemon peel

1 egg

2 teaspoons water

Confectioners' sugar

*I learned this recipe from my German grandmother Della and her sister Ella. They both claimed it as their original recipe. This bread has a high sugar content which causes it to be dark.*

1 package
    J. B. Dough
    Spicy Bread mix

1 egg

2 teaspoons water

## Spicy Herb Ring

Prepare bread mix following
J. B. Dough package instructions.
Set your machine on the dough mode
or on the manual setting.

Remove dough from bread machine.
Shape into long roll on lightly
floured surface. Shape into ring
on lightly greased baking sheet,
sealing ends together. Slash at
2-inch intervals.

Brush with mixture of egg and water.
Let rise in warm place for 1 hour.
Bake at 350 degrees for 25 to 30
minutes or until brown. Cool on wire
rack. Serve with your favorite soup
or chili and salad. Makes 1 Spicy
Herb Ring.

*Place in large round
basket or on bread
board. Arrange sprigs
of fresh herbs around
loaf and place a
container of your
favorite dip in center
of loaf. This makes a
great centerpiece for a
dinner party. Your
guests will love it and
the aroma is heavenly.*

# Holiday

## Gramma's Holiday Loaf

Prepare bread mix with warm water, buttermilk and 1 tablespoon honey following J. B. Dough package instructions. Set your machine on the dough mode or on the manual setting.

Remove dough from bread machine. Roll into 3/4-inch thick rectangle on lightly floured surface. Brush with melted butter.

Combine 1 tablespoon honey, maple syrup, orange juice, raisins, walnuts, orange rind and cinnamon in bowl; mix well. Spread over dough. Roll as for jelly roll; seal seam. Cut into 1-inch pieces.

Arrange enough slices, cut sides down, with sides touching to cover bottom of greased 10-inch tube pan. Arrange additional slices vertically around edge of pan and place remaining slices over first layer. Turn on oven for 1 minute; turn off oven. Place tube pan in warm oven. Let dough rise for 1 hour.

Turn on oven to 350 degrees. Bake for 25 to 30 minutes or until brown. Let stand in pan for 10 minutes. Invert onto wire rack to cool. Makes 1 Holiday Loaf.

1 package
J. B. Dough
Classic White
Bread mix

100 cc warm water

100 cc buttermilk

1 tablespoon honey

2 tablespoons melted butter

1 tablespoon honey

1 tablespoon maple syrup

1 tablespoon fresh orange juice

1/4 cup raisins

1/2 cup walnuts

2 teaspoons freshly grated orange rind

1 teaspoon cinnamon

1 package
   J. B. Dough
   Sweet Bread mix

1 egg

2 teaspoons water

Vanilla Sugar (page 89)

Candied cherries

Colored plastic wrap

Large bow

*Wrap in colored plastic wrap and place a large bow on tree trunk. Give as a holiday hostess gift.*

## Easy Christmas Tree

Prepare bread mix following J. B. Dough package instructions. Set your machine on the dough mode or on the manual setting.

Remove dough from bread machine. Roll dough into triangle with 12-inch base and 10-inch sides on lightly floured surface. Place on greased baking sheet. Make 2 cuts in base of triangle to form tree trunk; pull dough from trunk on each side. Make 4 diagonal cuts on each side to form branches. Let rise in warm place for 1 hour.

Brush with mixture of egg and water; sprinkle with Vanilla Sugar or plain sugar. Place a candied cherry at end of each branch. Bake at 350 degrees for 25 minutes. Remove to wire rack to cool completely. Makes 1 Christmas Tree.

# Holiday

## Cranberry-Nut Loaf

Prepare bread mix following J. B. Dough package instructions and add brown sugar. Set your machine on the dough mode or on the manual setting. Add cranberries and pecans at the beep according to your bread machine manufacturer's directions as for raisin bread.

Remove dough from bread machine. Place in greased 5x9-inch loaf pan. Refrigerate, covered with paper towel, overnight. Place uncovered loaf pan in oven.

Turn oven on to 350 degrees. Bake for 25 to 30 minutes or until golden brown. Remove to wire rack to cool. Frost with mixture of confectioners' sugar and milk or just garnish with sprinkle of confectioners' sugar. Makes 1 Cranberry-Nut Loaf.

1 package J. B. Dough Whole Earth Bread mix

1 tablespoon brown sugar

1/4 cup dried cranberries

1/4 cup chopped pecans

1/2 cup confectioners' sugar

4 teaspoons milk

*Give Cranberry-Nut Loaf as a Thanksgiving Day hostess gift.*

1 package
J. B. Dough
Sweet Bread mix

Mincemeat Filling

1 tablespoon flour

1 tablespoon sugar

2 teaspoons butter

## Mincemeat Ladder Loaf

Prepare bread mix following J. B. Dough package instructions. Set your machine on the dough mode or on the manual setting.

Remove dough from bread machine. Roll into 9x12-inch rectangle on lightly floured surface. Place on greased baking sheet. Spread Mincemeat Filling down center of rectangle.

Make 3-inch cuts from edge toward center at 1-inch intervals. Fold alternate strips diagonally over filling; press ends to seal. Sprinkle with mixture of flour, sugar and butter. Let rise in warm place for 1 hour. Bake at 350 degrees for 25 minutes. Makes 1 Mincemeat Ladder Loaf.

1/2 cup mincemeat

1/2 cup applesauce

1 tablespoon water

## Mincemeat Filling

Combine mincemeat, applesauce and water in small microwave-safe bowl. Microwave on High for about 2 minutes or until thickened, stirring several times. Let stand until cool.

## Easter Egg Bread Centerpiece

| |
|---|
| 1 package J. B. Dough Classic White Bread mix |
| 1 egg yolk |
| 2 teaspoons grated lemon rind |
| 1/2 teaspoon ground anise |
| 5 tinted hard-boiled eggs |
| 1 egg |
| 2 teaspoons water |

Prepare bread mix following J. B. Dough package instructions, using mixture of egg yolk and enough water to measure 200 cc or 7/8 cup for liquid. Add lemon rind and anise. Set your machine on the dough mode or on the manual setting.

Remove dough from bread machine. Divide into 2 equal portions. Shape each into rope; twist together. Shape into circle on lightly greased baking sheet; seal ends together. Make 5 indentations in dough. Place tinted egg in each indentation. Let dough rise for 1 hour. Remove eggs.

Brush ring with mixture of egg and water. Bake at 350 degrees for 25 to 30 minutes or until golden brown. Cool on wire rack. Replace eggs in indentations. Makes 1 Easter Egg Bread.

*Wrap in colored plastic wrap and decorate with a large bow and cluster of dried flowers. May shape into long braid instead of ring. Wrap in plastic wrap and tie both ends with satin bows.*

*For tinted egg glaze, beat 2 egg yolks with 2 teaspoons water. Spoon into 4 custard cups. Tint with food colorings and brush on eggs.*

# Specialties

# Specialties

## Basil-Cream Cheese Bread

Slice loaf into halves lengthwise. Beat cream cheese, basil, garlic powder, butter and Parmesan cheese in mixing bowl until combined. Spread mixture on bottom half of loaf. Top with remaining half.

Wrap baguette in foil. Place on baking sheet. Bake at 350 degrees for 20 minutes or until heated through. Cut into slices. Serve warm. Makes 12 servings.

> 1 loaf
>   J. B. Dough
>   Vienna Bread
>
> 3 ounces cream cheese, softened
>
> 1/2 teaspoon basil
>
> 1/4 teaspoon garlic powder
>
> 2 tablespoons butter, softened
>
> 2 tablespoons grated Parmesan cheese

1 loaf
  J. B. Dough
  California Sour
  Dough Bread,
  cut into 8 slices

1/4 cup butter

1 clove of garlic

4 ounces feta cheese,
  crumbled

2 tablespoons calamata
  olives, pitted,
  chopped

Parsley flakes to taste

# Feta-Olive Sour Dough Bread

Place bread slices on baking sheet. Broil for 2 to 3 minutes or until brown on 1 side; turn slices. Combine butter and garlic in microwave-safe dish. Microwave for 1 minute or until butter melts; discard garlic.

Brush over bread. Top with feta cheese and olives; sprinkle with parsley flakes. Broil for 1 to 3 minutes or until cheese melts and edges of bread are brown. Serve with soup or cut into smaller pieces for an appetizer. Makes 8 servings.

# Specialties

## Fried Garlic Toast

Slice bread into desired thickness; cut slices into halves. Combine butter and olive oil in skillet. Cook over medium heat until butter melts. Stir in garlic.

Dip both sides of bread slices in butter mixture. Cook over medium heat until brown on both sides. Top with cheese. Cook until cheese melts. Makes 12 servings.

1 loaf
  J. B. Dough
  Vienna Bread

1/4 cup butter

2 tablespoons olive oil

1 clove of garlic, sliced

1/2 cup shredded
  mozzarella cheese

## Great Garlic Bread

Slice loaf into halves lengthwise. Combine butter, garlic, Parmesan cheese, parsley flakes, basil and paprika in bowl; mix well. Spread mixture evenly on each bread half. Place on baking sheet. Broil until brown. Makes 12 servings.

1 loaf
  J. B. Dough
  Vienna Bread

1/2 cup butter, softened

5 to 6 cloves of garlic,
  finely chopped

3 tablespoons grated
  Parmesan cheese

1 teaspoon parsley
  flakes

1/2 teaspoon basil

1/4 teaspoon paprika

1 package
J. B. Dough
Classic White
Bread mix

2 tablespoons butter

1 clove of garlic

$1/2$ teaspoon onion
powder

3 tablespoons grated
Parmesan cheese

# Garlic-Cheese Rolls

Prepare bread mix following J. B. Dough package instructions. Set your machine on the dough mode or on the manual setting.

Remove dough from bread machine. Divide dough into 16 portions. Arrange in buttered round baking dish.

Microwave butter and garlic in microwave-safe dish for 30 seconds or until butter melts; discard garlic. Drizzle over dough; sprinkle with onion powder and Parmesan cheese.

Let rise in warm place for 1 hour. Bake at 350 degrees for 25 to 30 minutes or until brown.
Makes 16 servings.

# S p e c i a l t i e s

## Merrilou's Cheese Bread

Cut loaf into slices diagonally, cutting to but not through the bottom. Place 1 slice of cheese in each cut. Drizzle each slice with mixture of butter, onion, mustard, poppy seeds and seasoned salt.

Place loaf in foil shell; do not cover top. Bake at 350 degrees for 30 minutes. Makes 12 servings.

1 loaf
 J. B. Dough
 Vienna Bread

8 ounces Swiss cheese,
 thinly sliced

1/2 cup melted butter

2 tablespoons ( or
 more) chopped
 onion

1 tablespoon Dijon
 mustard

1 tablespoon poppy
 seeds

1/2 teaspoon seasoned
 salt

*Merrilou serves this bread at bridge parties with a salad.*

*May substitute Dutch mustard or any spicy mustard for Dijon mustard.*

1 loaf
  J. B. Dough
  Country Rye Bread

$1/2$ cup grated
  Parmesan cheese

$1/4$ cup mayonnaise

$1/4$ cup finely chopped
  green onions

2 tablespoons sour
  cream

1 tablespoon chopped
  parsley

# Parmesan Rye Bread

Cut loaf into 14 equal slices, cutting to but not through the bottom. Beat Parmesan cheese, mayonnaise, green onions, sour cream and parsley in mixing bowl until combined. Spread every other slice with cheese mixture. Wrap in foil. Bake at 350 degrees for 20 minutes. Makes 14 servings.

# Specialties

## Onion-Dill-Fennel Sticks

1 package
J. B. Dough
Onion Dill
Bread mix

1 tablespoon olive oil

1 teaspoon fennel seeds

Water

Kosher salt to taste

Prepare bread mix following J. B. Dough package instructions. Add olive oil with liquid ingredients. Add fennel seeds with dry ingredients. Set your machine on the dough mode or on the manual setting.

Remove dough from bread machine. Divide dough into 2 portions. Divide each portion into 10 pieces. Roll each piece into a rope with floured hands.

Place on greased baking sheet. Brush with water; sprinkle with salt. Let rise in warm place for 30 minutes.

Bake at 350 degrees for 12 to 16 minutes or until brown. Serve warm. Makes 20 servings.

1 package
J. B. Dough
Potato Bread mix

1 tablespoon sugar

3 tablespoons melted
butter

2 tablespoons chopped
fresh parsley

1/2 teaspoon basil

1/4 teaspoon garlic
powder

2 tablespoons chopped
fresh chives

# Herb-Swirled Potato Rolls

Prepare bread mix following
J. B. Dough package instructions. Add
sugar with dry ingredients. Set your
machine on the dough mode or on
the manual setting.

Remove dough from bread machine.
Roll into rectangle on lightly floured
surface. Drizzle with 3 tablespoons
melted butter; sprinkle with parsley,
basil, garlic powder and chives.

Roll as for jelly roll, sealing edge and
ends. Cut into 1-inch slices. Place on
greased baking sheet. Let rise in warm
place for 1 hour. Bake at 350 degrees
for 25 minutes; brush with additional
melted butter. Makes 8 servings.

# Specialties

## Soup Bowls

Prepare bread mix following J. B. Dough package instructions. Set your machine on the dough mode or on the manual setting.

Remove dough from bread machine. Shape into 3 round loaves. Place on greased baking sheet. Crisscross dough with sharp knife; brush with mixture of egg and water.

Let rise in warm place for 1 hour. Bake at 350 degrees for 25 minutes. Remove to wire rack to cool completely. Cut top from bread; remove center carefully, leaving 1-inch shell.

Place bread shells and tops on baking sheet. Brush inside of shells with olive oil. Bake for 10 to 15 minutes or until light brown. Spoon your favorite soup, chili or stew inside shell; cover with bread top. Garnish with fresh herbs. Makes 3 bowls.

1 package
   J. B. Dough
   Vienna Bread mix

1 egg, beaten

2 teaspoons water

Olive oil

*I like to serve this with a creamy-style soup and Caesar salad. A creamy soup holds up better in the bowls.*

1 loaf
   J. B. Dough
   Spicy Bread

2 tablespoons olive oil

1 tablespoon melted
   butter

Garlic salt to taste

Assorted herbs to taste

Parmesan cheese
   (optional)

*Store leftover bread in
the freezer to make
croutons.*

# Croutons

Trim crust from bread; cut into cubes. Arrange bread cubes on baking sheet. Combine olive oil and butter in bowl; mix well. Drizzle half the mixture over bread cubes. Sprinkle with garlic salt and your favorite herbs. Bake at 350 degrees for 10 minutes; stir. Drizzle remaining olive oil mixture over cubes. Bake for 5 minutes. Cool. Sprinkle with Parmesan cheese. Store in glass container. Serve with soups and salads. Makes 16 servings.

# S p e c i a l t i e s

## Johnny's Herb Garden Dip

Combine garlic and water in microwave-safe dish. Microwave for 40 seconds; drain and finely chop garlic. Combine garlic, cream cheese, herbs and half and half in mixing bowl. Beat until blended. Serve with toasted bread pieces.

1 clove of garlic

1 tablespoon water

8 ounces light cream cheese, softened

2 tablespoons finely chopped fresh herbs

1 tablespoon half and half

*May use any fresh herbs, such as pineapple sage, garlic chives, lemon balm and basil. May substitute 1 teaspoon dried herbs for 2 tablespoons chopped fresh herbs.*

*May substitute whipping cream or lowfat milk for half and half.*

1 package
  J. B. Dough
  Vienna Bread mix

6 tablespoons melted
  butter

1 cup chopped pecans

1 tablespoon peanut oil

Salt to taste

4 ounces cream cheese,
  softened

1 large red Delicious
  apple, cut into 24
  slices

8 ounces Brie, cut into
  24 pieces

24 pecan halves

# Apple-Brie Appetizer

Prepare bread mix following
J. B. Dough package instructions. Set
your machine on the dough mode or
on the manual setting.

Remove dough from bread machine.
Divide dough into 2 portions.
Shape into 2 baguettes. Place on
baking sheet. Let rise in warm place
for 1 hour.

Bake at 350 degrees until brown.
Remove to wire rack to cool. Cut
into 24 slices. Arrange slices on
nonstick baking sheet.

Bake at 400 degrees until light brown
on 1 side. Turn slices over; brush
with melted butter. Bake until brown.

Process 1 cup chopped pecans and
peanut oil in food processor until
smooth. Season with salt. Spread
toasted bread slices with cream
cheese. Arrange apple slice, Brie and
pecan mixture on each slice. Top
with pecan half. Bake in moderate
oven for 1 to 2 minutes or just until
cheese melts. Makes 24 servings.

# Specialties

## Amaretto Butter

Cream butter, confectioners' sugar and Amaretto in mixer bowl until light and fluffy. Stir in chopped almonds. Spoon into serving bowl or crock.

1/2 cup butter, softened

2 tablespoons confectioners' sugar

1 1/2 tablespoons Amaretto

3 tablespoons finely chopped toasted almonds

## Green Herb Butter

Cream butter in mixer bowl until light and fluffy. Add spinach purée, parsley and chives; mix well. Serve on lettuce leaf.

1/2 cup butter, softened

1 teaspoon spinach purée

1 teaspoon finely chopped parsley

1/2 teaspoon finely chopped chives

## Mushroom Butter

Combine all ingredients in bowl, stirring until spreading consistency.

1/2 cup butter, softened

2 tablespoons sautéed mushrooms

Lemon juice to taste

1/4 teaspoon each garlic and onion powder

Confectioners' sugar to taste

Salt and white pepper to taste

1/2 cup unsalted
  butter, softened

2 tablespoons pure
  maple syrup, at
  room temperature

1 tablespoon finely
  chopped pecans

# Maple-Pecan Butter

Beat butter and maple syrup in mixing
bowl until creamy. Stir in pecans.
Spoon into crock or serving bowl.

1/2 cup butter, softened

2 tablespoons
  confectioners' sugar

1 teaspoon grated
  orange rind

1 teaspoon orange juice

# Orange Butter

Cream butter, confectioners' sugar,
orange rind and orange juice in
mixing bowl until creamy. Spoon into
crock or serving bowl. Serve at
room temperature.

1/2 cup unsalted
  butter, softened

2 tablespoons
  confectioners' sugar

2 tablespoons
  strawberry jam, at
  room temperature

# Strawberry Butter

Beat butter, confectioners' sugar
and strawberry jam in mixing bowl
until blended. Spoon into crock
or serving bowl.

*Homemade strawberry
jam is preferred.*

# Specialties

## Apricot-Date Cheese Spread

Combine ricotta cheese and yogurt in bowl; mix well. Spoon mixture into cheesecloth. Drain over bowl in refrigerator overnight; discard liquid. Combine cheese mixture, confectioners' sugar, apricots and dates in bowl; mix well. Serve with sourdough bread. Store, covered, in refrigerator for 1 week.

1 cup low-fat ricotta cheese

1/4 cup nonfat plain yogurt

1 tablespoon confectioners' sugar

2 tablespoons finely chopped dried apricots

2 tablespoons chopped dates

## Garlic-Cheese Spread

Beat cream cheese, Old English cheese, Roka cheese, garlic powder and onion powder in mixing bowl until smooth. Serve with toast points.

8 ounces cream cheese, softened

1   5-ounce jar Old English cheese, at room temperature

1   5-ounce jar Roka bleu cheese, at room temperature

1/4 teaspoon garlic powder

1/4 teaspoon onion powder

1   12 ounce block
    havarti cheese

1 teaspoon Dijon
    mustard

1 teaspoon parsley
    flakes

1/2 teaspoon chives

1/4 teaspoon dillweed

1/4 teaspoon basil

## Herb-Cheese Spread

Place cheese in ovenproof dish.
Spread with Dijon mustard; sprinkle
with parsley, chives, dillweed and
basil. Bake at 300 degrees for 15
minutes. Serve with toasted bread
cubes. Garnish serving platter with
grape leaves.

8 ounces mild goat
    cheese

1/2 cup butter, softened

1 large clove of garlic,
    mashed

1 teaspoon salt

1/4 cup chopped
    toasted pistachio
    nuts

2 tablespoons chopped
    chives

1 loaf
    J. B. Dough
    Vienna or
    Sour Dough Bread,
    sliced, toasted

## Pistachio-Goat Cheese Spread

Combine goat cheese, butter, garlic,
salt, pistachio nuts and chives in
bowl; mix well. Serve with toasted
bread and a good bottle of red wine.

# Specialties

## Roasted Garlic and Bean Spread

Place garlic in small baking dish. Bake at 400 degrees for 15 minutes or until garlic is tender but not brown. Cool. Discard skins. Combine garlic, white beans, lemon juice and olive oil in food processor container. Process until blended. Add parsley, pepper and green onions. Process just until blended. Serve with J. B. Dough Three Seed Bread, Six Grain Bread, Pumpernickel Bread or Country Rye Bread. Cut bread slices into small wedges. Place on baking sheet. Toast on both sides until brown.

12 cloves of garlic

2 16-ounce cans white beans, rinsed, drained

1/4 cup lemon juice

1 tablespoon olive oil

1 tablespoon chopped fresh parsley

Pepper to taste

1/4 cup chopped green onions

## Strawberry Cream Cheese

Combine cream cheese, confectioners' sugar and strawberries in bowl; mix well. Spoon into crock. Serve on toasted bread or sourdough bread. Store, covered, in refrigerator for 1 week.

8 ounces cream cheese, softened

1/4 cup confectioners' sugar

1/2 cup sliced strawberries

1 cup water

1/2 cup dry mustard

2 tablespoons cornstarch

1/2 teaspoon tarragon

1/4 teaspoon salt

1/4 cup honey

2 tablespoons cider vinegar

1 tablespoon canola oil

*Give as a gift accompanied with baguette or pumpernickel bread or with a smoked luncheon meat roll.*

# Honey Mustard

Combine water, mustard, cornstarch, tarragon and salt in saucepan; mix well. Cook until thickened and bubbly, stirring constantly. Cook for 2 minutes, stirring constantly. Stir in honey, vinegar and oil. Cool, covered with plastic wrap. Spoon into decorative container or small jar.

6 ounces cream cheese, softened

1 cup finely chopped pecans

1/4 teaspoon garlic powder

4 drops of hot sauce

1/8 teaspoon Worcestershire sauce

1/8 teaspoon salt

1/8 teaspoon pepper

# Pecan Log

Beat cream cheese, pecans, garlic powder, hot sauce, Worcestershire sauce, salt and pepper in mixer bowl until combined. Shape into roll. Chill, wrapped in waxed paper. Cut into thin slices. Serve with thinly sliced and toasted J. B. Dough bread.

# Index

# I n d e x

# I n d e x

For ordering information on

The J. B. Dough Company product line

and your nearest distributor

**Call 1-800-528-6222**

or write

The J. B. Dough Company

P.O. Box 557

St. Joseph, MI 49085-0557

(616) 983-1025

Fax (616) 983-6532

$M$y wish for you is that your house will be blessed with happiness that many only dream of, and never quite reach.  If only they knew the secret—it's found in the magic mix of a warm kitchen, the aroma of fresh bread, and the delight that surrounds the smiles of love in every bite.

We would love to hear from you—whether it's a question, an idea to share, or a wonderful story from your hearth.  Please write us at:

The J. B. Dough Company

P.O. Box 557

St. Joseph, MI 49085-0557